Strategies and Techniques to Beat the Competition

Selling Office Products Successfully

TERRILL KLETT

DIGITAL PUBLISHING

St. Charles, Illinois

Published by DIGITAL PUBLISHING
6N830 Foxborough Road
St. Charles, IL 60175

Publisher's Cataloging-in-Publication Data
Klett, Terrill.
    Selling office products successfully: strategies and techniques to beat the
    competition / Terrill Klett – St. Charles, IL: Digital Publishing, 2001.
        p.   ill.   cm.
    ISBN 0-9708288-0-2

    1. Selling–office equipment and supplies–handbooks, manuals, etc.
    2. Selling–handbooks, manuals, etc. I. Title.
HF5439 .04   2001   2001-86779
658.810–dc21   CIP

05 04 03 02 01 ▼ 5 4 3 2 1

Project coordination by Jenkins *Group@Bookpublishing.com*

Printed in the United States of America

Selling Office
Products
Successfully

Contents

Acknowledgments 7

Introduction 9

Ready

Chapter 1 Solid As a Rock or
Rock Bottom?...Choice 15

Chapter 2 It's Only Just Begun...Education 20

Chapter 3 "Huh, What Did You Say?"...
Listening 24

Chapter 4 "I-I-I" Is a "No-No-No"...Teamwork 27

Chapter 5 "I Just Had It; Where Did It Go?"...
Organization 31

Chapter 6 Positively Positive...Attitude 36

Understand

Chapter 7 Telemarketing 43

Chapter 8 Cold Calling 49

Chapter 9   Qualifying   54

Chapter 10   Objections   60

Chapter 11   Demonstrations   64

Chapter 12   Closing   71

Chapter 13   Persistence   77

Differentiate

Chapter 14   Creativity   83

Chapter 15   Communicating Effectively   90

Chapter 16   Major Account Selling   95

Chapter 17   Gaining Additional Gross Profit   100

Chapter 18   Defeating Time   105

Chapter 19   Price War   112

Yourself

Chapter 20   The Painful Journey to Success   119

Chapter 21   Got a "Match"–Sales Management   123

Chapter 22   Gaining Customer Loyalty   129

Chapter 23   Complacency   134

Chapter 24   Are You "RUDY" for the Future?   139

Acknowledgments

To my lovely wife, Karen, who was patient and supportive throughout my research, and for the hours she spent rewriting each draft.

To my boys, Corbin and Brody, who mostly understood that Dad couldn't play sometimes because he had made a commitment to make the salesperson's life just a little easier.

To my parents, Fred and Joanne, who instilled in me that giving and receiving love is what really matters in life.

To my eight brothers and one sister, who have given me enough inspiration and life memories to write ten books. From oldest to youngest: Jeff, Fred, Kyle, Jaren, Jon, Derek, Matthew, Stephanie, and Benjamin.

To my mentors and friends, Jim Van De Veire and Fred Eddy, who kept me in this industry with their leadership skills and personal attention.

Last, a special thanks to those involved with everything from design and graphics to lending a few helpful hints: Steve Smith, Dean Folts, Keith Draper, Jeff Smith, and George Yanik.

Thanks a million and I love you all!

Introduction

Every day in sales we are asked to jump through fire burning hoops. We are told to do it with a positive attitude, a charming smile, and with the desire to be the best at what we do. We are seldom given the necessary tools or time, but we are pressured to make our quota that seems to be just a "little too high" every month. Successful selling in the office products industry requires you to be **R**eady every day with strong interpersonal skills. Concurrent with these are having the knowledge to **U**nderstand each phase of the selling cycle. The real success in your career will be in gaining the advanced skills to **D**ifferentiate yourself from the competition so that the prospect buys from you. Finally, no one will do it for you—the responsibility lies within **Y**ourself! In a challenging industry we must be as multifunctional as the products we sell. With this in mind, RUDY and this book were born!

Ready – Understand – Differentiate – Yourself

RUDY is the consummate sales person. RUDY has big ears to listen and large feet to walk the extra mile. Colorful and wearing a smile as wide as a river, RUDY has developed all the skills necessary to be the "Top Dog."

The world did not need another sales book; our profession has been inundated with books on the subject. However, the office automation industry did need a book specifically designed for it, especially since technology has changed so quickly to digital. Even the names of products have changed overnight; for example, the copier is also referred to as an imaging system, multifunctional product (MFP), or digital system, to name a few. Traditional one-dimensional office machines such as the printer and facsimile have evolved into multi-faceted workstations. The way we walk and talk today has experienced a 360-degree turnaround.

Salespeople and managers are extremely busy today so each chapter is short and "right to the good stuff." There are twenty-four chapters so that the really busy salesperson can concentrate on one chapter for every business day and be finished in a month! The book is designed so that you don't have to read each chapter in order for the next one to make sense. Feel free to skip around depending on your level of ability and need for the week. Each chapter closes with a motivational tip from RUDY that summarizes the main point of the chapter.

For those of you who are just beginning your "adventure" in this terrific industry, you'll enjoy the people, products, and daily challenges. If you have already been contaminated with "toner in your blood," keep your enthusiasm and professionalism up every day to keep this fast moving industry enjoyable.

My hope is that everyone who sells office products will utilize the information outlined in this book to increase their sales. The successful salesperson needs to get out of the old concept of "moving boxes" to becoming a "solutions provider." Good luck "jumping through the fire-burning hoops!"

Ready

The initial and on-going challenge of office equipment sales can be summed up with one key word: *Ready!* One guarantee in this business is that every day something new (and hopefully exciting) will happen. You will encounter multiple personalites and your attitude has to be positive in every circumstance. The customer expects you to be not only a perfect listener but to be educated in your field. The smile on your face is not only for the customer but also for your teammates back at the office. When the next crisis arises you will have to be organized enough to handle it swiftly and accurately. Every day you wake up there will be another challenge with critical choices to make. Are you ready?

Chapter 1

Solid As a Rock or Rock Bottom?...Choice

Virtually every sales office has a disorganized section of old, torn, and tattered sales materials and books. While sifting through a pile last year, I was amazed to find a fantastic book by an ex-copier salesman, Hal Becker, entitled *Can I Have 5 Minutes of Your Time?* What amazed me was the fact that in his second year of selling copiers for Xerox he found himself residing in the number one position in the country out of 11,000 sales-people. Why *wouldn't* anyone want to read this book? With a record like Mr. Becker's, it's pretty easy to make the decision to at least skim the information he has to offer in attempt to better yourself and grasp a few of the strategies that worked for him.

I wish that I were packing a load of credentials similar to Becker, Zig Ziglar, Brian Tracey, or Tom Hopkins. The reality is, I am not. This is why what you are about to read is more geared toward the average salesperson, because I'm basically the same salesperson as you! If you profiled the most average salesperson eighteen years ago, chances are you'd include me in your list, without any special notations beside my name—just a regular guy.

In my second year I did climb out of the near basement position to the number *five* ranking, not bad all things considered, though there were a total of ten of us!

Throughout the years I have devoted quite some time to studying what the experts inside as well as outside the office products industry had to say. I read their books, listened to tapes, took notes (which I recorded on my laptop by subject), and eventually won some of the sales contests locally and nationally that took me to Hawaii, Germany, and Japan to name a few places. As far as Becker and I are concerned, we did end up with the same result—a book. The types of books we have written, though, are radically different. This book is not about what I did, but about what *you* are capable of doing. My personal story is briefly told in this first chapter, to set the stage.

After completing college I did not choose to go into sales immediately. After all, my life was just beginning and I had plenty of time before I needed to adopt a more serious mission in life. I had spent all of my life in the beautiful but extremely cold state of Wisconsin and had visions of myself frolicking in the warmth and fun that California and Florida had to offer. After all, sales wasn't a big deal and since I'm basically a nice guy with a respectable personality and competitive spirit, being successful in this environment would be a piece of cake...or so I thought. I believed that I could just join in at any time, and with a smooth transition.

As all good things must come to an end, I felt after a few years that my sun-frolicking, carefree days must come to a close. I moved back to Beloit, Wisconsin, and then went south once again, but this time only a hundred miles which landed me in the big city of Chicago. I just knew I would be successful in sales.

Copier sales seemed intriguing after a variety of interviews and prospective sales possibilities, so I started on the best day of the year, my twenty-eighth birthday. It was October 1, 1984, and it was one of those gorgeous fall days in Chicago. I was burning with excitement! I was now part of the greatest profession in the world because nothing happens until something is sold.

The initial ninety days went all right. I ran into a few deals and got my feet wet. With the arrival of the new year and the sense of renewal and goal-setting it brings, I was excited. The timing was perfect, because I had worked my ninety-day "training period" and was now ready to show my stuff. But January is a long, dark, cold month in Chicago and it seemed to be never-ending. For whatever reason, none of the prospects were buying from me and this fact was reinforced on the Wednesday night month-end meeting by a big zero ($0) for sales totals next to my name. On this same evening I was to demonstrate a 55 cpm copier to the team and I remember them saying, "We are not going to be easy on you now because your training period is over." The demonstration did not go well and I found it extremely difficult taking the criticism from my peers. The old maxim "Nobody loves you when you're down and out" fit my situation perfectly.

Before this week had even begun I was depressed, knowing that I had no money or even a credit card, was driving around a station wagon (not good for a single guy at that time), and was failing at what I thought should be easy. I was sick of wearing the same two cheap suits and shoes, and now my teammates were pounding me. The strangest feeling came upon me during my demonstration and I realized that I was about to cry. I had endured more than a few fights with my eight brothers while growing up and had wrestled in many tournaments throughout high school and college and none of these had made me cry. When I realized that tears were about to fall I abruptly halted my demonstration, quit my job (in my mind), and dashed out the back door to my stupid station wagon. It was there that I felt it would be safe to let the tears of defeat roll down my face.

Suddenly my car door was opened and I found my sales manager, Don Kroopkin, standing outside. Don was a caring gentleman and had some kind words to offer. I remember him telling me, **"Sometimes you need to hit rock bottom before you can go up."** This statement made sense to me, and realizing that there really was nowhere to go but up I decided to stick it out and show up the following morning. The darkest hour is only sixty minutes long so I was hopeful that there would be some light appearing.

Looking back, I now realize that this was the best thing that could have happened to me. This was my wake-up call. The loneliest people are those who no longer believe in themselves, and I did not want to be lonely.

I soon realized that, up until now, I had accepted a job but had not committed to the opportunity before me. A job means "Just Over Broke," which is where you will be if you don't make the right *choice*. You have the choice to make the footsteps or to follow them. Success does not happen overnight, but the choice to become successful can. Make the choice to do what you are supposed to do when you are supposed to do it, even though you don't quite want to at the time. I quickly learned that you don't wait for your ship to come in; it never will. You are responsible for making the choice to swim out to your ship. Success will not show up at the dock by chance.

In sales we are faced with choices every day. Indeed, life in general requires us to make more choices in three months than our grandparents had to make in their lifetimes. Patrick Henry is the only human being I know of who managed to narrow his choices down to two: "Give me liberty or give me death." In a way, we are also confronted with only two choices: To succeed or to fail. You can choose to snooze and lose tomorrow or you can commit yourself to jump through the fire-burning hoop with a smile that says, "I'll be number one." Finally, if all goes well, you can even choose to write a book!

RUDY **Says:** The only limitations we have are the ones we place on ourselves. You have the choice to think you can or to think you can't. Either way, you will be right. Remember, the *will* must be stronger than the *skill*.

Chapter 2

It's Only Just Begun...Education

WHEN YOU START COLLEGE YOU ARE TOLD THAT IF YOU steal from one person, it is plagiarism; if you steal from ten it is research; and if you steal from hundreds, you are a scholar. There is no excuse for not being a scholar in the office products industry! The goal of *Selling Office Products Successfully* is that you will steal the information, reformat it into your own words if necessary, and use the material to increase your sales! Each chapter will include practical strategies that can be employed throughout your sales career. Not all strategies will appeal to everyone, so go ahead and be a picky thief.

One of the most difficult tasks is to just take the time to educate yourself. Only three percent of corporate America gets involved in continuing education while on the job, and sixty percent of the population never reads another book after formal education. Perhaps the most valuable result of all education is developing the discipline to make yourself do the things you have to do, when they ought to be done, whether you like to do them or not. One strategy is to set up a firm date and time each week to read, study, or practice something that will give you a competitive edge. Some suggestions are over lunch, immediately before or after work, or one night a week instead of turning on the television or surfing the Internet.

Determining where to find information to "steal" is easy in the information age. You have access to just about any information on any product or company. All of the suppliers/distributors/manufacturers have an Internet site and many provide specifications of every product. There are numerous industry reports, Internet sites, buyer's guides, and computer disks on the competition. Beyond that you can buy a cassette tape or book on any subject of sales imaginable. No excuse is acceptable for not having the resources because all it takes is a library card!

Today it is more important than ever to have an edge on the competition. In his 1956 book *Organization Man*, William White Jr. said, "Be loyal to the company and the company will be loyal to you." Those were the days of lifetime employment and steady promotions. Forward the clock thirty years to 1996 to an article in the Wall Street Journal that stated, "No one is going to take care of you but yourself." This doesn't mean you should be selfish and abandon your team; it simply means that in today's marketplace anything can happen with an employer so prepare yourself to be so valuable that you become invincible.

There is an old adage that goes, *"To learn you must teach."* When my oldest son, Corbin, was seven, he began taking piano lessons that cost thirteen dollars. Twelve went to the teacher and one of the dollars went to him the next day to teach me the lesson he was taught. This made him concentrate more and by explaining what he had learned, he also comprehended his lesson much better. Your payback for taking the time to learn will be much more than his one dollar with the extra commissions you will earn!

Salespeople have the tendency to avoid putting themselves on the spot in order to teach others, but by doing so they utilize a great learning skill. Take some of the new information you read in the next few weeks and volunteer to share it at the next sales meeting. If you are a sales manager or owner, ask the sales team to pinpoint one area in which they would like to improve themselves. Whatever subject they choose, assign them to research and present it. Remember that "To learn you must teach." Putting someone on the spot in order to improve their career will benefit everyone.

Educating yourself can also be a fun task. On the last day of a recent BTA (Business Technology Association) show in Las Vegas, Nevada, I went to every manufacturer's booth and asked a simple question: "What is the key to selling high end digital imaging systems?" I received a few puzzled looks but I did gather a lot of great answers from the industry experts. Then I wrote the twenty best ones down and shared them in a series of meetings and I seemed like the ultimate expert! Stealing from the competitors was easy. When you ask others their opinions it honors them and you will usually get some professional and creative answers. The best sources are within your own dealership and, believe it or not, your own customers.

Professors on the whole live longer than any other professional group. One theory for this is that they keep stretching their minds and tend to immerse themselves in mentally stimulating atmospheres long after retirement. They also have the willingness to be trained. When I was thirteen years old my dad used to take my two older brothers and me to his Prudential Insurance office and would use his blackboard to teach us exciting subjects like selling Ordinary and Whole Life insurance policies. Dad's effort was valiant but as a new teenager my mind was on other things.

As an adult, try to get the most out of every educational session. The importance sometimes lies in the fact of not what you learned but the identification of how much you don't know along with how much you need to learn. If you haven't learned or rein-forced at least one idea a day, you've wasted a whole day.

"Discernment" may be the most important educational word today. It means recognizing and understanding what is right. Just because someone said something doesn't mean they are right. By the same token, believing doesn't make something so either. Make sure you verify information that is passed on to you by your own research or by asking others their understanding on the subject.

Graduating from school was not the end of your education; it was only the beginning. Some day retirement will sneak upon you so be prepared now by expanding your mind, industry knowledge, and earnings by taking time to become a "good" thief. The train-ing you receive will only be as good as the commitment you make. Make sure the commitment stays at a high level and take the infor-mation you hear or read and put it into your words and personality to make it practical. Remember, your thirst for more sales skills should expire when your need for oxygen expires.

"When I get a little money I buy books; and if any is left I buy food and clothes."

ERASMUS

"If you are planning for a year, sow rice; if you are planning for a decade, plant trees; if you are planning for a lifetime, educate people."

CHINESE PROVERB

RUDY **Says:** You need to share what you learn so that there will be more to earn. Education should be a concern so make that commitment and take your turn.

Chapter 3

"Huh, What Did You Say?"...Listening

"**S**HUT UP AND LISTEN" SEEMED TO BE ABOUT THE ONLY training we got after the age of five when it came to listening. Now that the digital era has overloaded us with information, we have become too busy to listen and it may be costing us a lot of business! Many years ago General Electric purchasing agents had a meeting to determine the biggest reason for loss of sales. The outcome of this investigation showed that by far the number one factor that resulted in lost sales concerned the art of listening. The listening skills of the sales force were simply lacking.

The fact is, we were given two ears and only one mouth to remind us to listen twice as much as we talk. With changes in technology we're probably listening more, but only because we don't know what we're talking about as much as we used to. Listening skills can be improved with a little practice and patience, even when you do know what you're talking about!

Look back at your last few appointments and ask yourself if you listened twice as much as you talked. One strategy to show the customer you are listening is to repeat back the question or objection they have given you. This also will clarify what was said and give customers a chance to change or answer it themselves.

Why is listening so difficult? You would think that the odds of perfecting this skill would be 50-50, after all, we are either listening or talking. Most people can listen at a speed of 600 words per minute but can only speak at 125 to 150 words per minute. It's not all that easy so practice the following suggestions to better your skills in this area:

1. Ask good questions. Did you ever notice that if you know how to ask a good question and then take time to listen for the response, you'll never run out of good conversation? (Don't hesitate to utilize the word "why" if you aren't able to generate a lot of questions.)

2. Concentrate on genuine concern, not just conversation. Listen with your eyes and heart.

3. Wait for your turn. Don't interrupt.

4. Concentrate on what is being said rather than thinking ahead to what you will contribute next.

It is also important to establish good listening skills in others— you want the customer to listen to you. Since customers are very important persons (VIPS), give them the VIPS listening treatment!

Volume–express yourself using various volume levels in your voice

Inflection–emphasize key words

Pace–slow down/speed up

Silence–this will create some surprises, especially when coming from a salesperson. "Silence is Golden," so be silent and bring home the gold!

Good listeners also make good friends. Good friends know other good friends, who in turn may need to purchase precisely that product you are selling! Not only are good listeners popular everywhere, they also possess a wealth of knowledge because they have learned so much!

> When listening be like...
> The wise old owl who sat on an oak
> The more he saw the less he spoke
> The less he spoke the more he heard
> Why aren't we all like that wise old bird?
>> Anonymous

(If you have kids you probably get a lot of these poems.)

> *"We only hear half of what is said to us, understand only half of that, believe only half of that and remember only half of that."*
>> MIGON MCLAUGHIN

> *"The wise man has long ears, big eyes, and a short tongue."*
>> RUSSIAN PROVERB

RUDY Says: The highest form of courtesy is listening. Listening to everyone in your office with an open mind will be a good start to forming a successful team!

Chapter 4

"I-I-I" Is a "No-No-No"...Teamwork

SELLING AND SPORTS FOR BOTH MEN AND WOMEN HAVE A number of common characteristics. There's the competition, the victory, and the defeat. Good sportsmanship is vital to any winning team, and as part of a sales team the characteristic most specific to this "sport" would be the ability to work as a good team member.

Training has always seemed to focus on either technology or product. When sales skills are given it is usually in regard to the selling cycle. We are told throughout our sales careers to "be good listeners" or to "be good teammates" but no one ever trains us on the "how to"! The illustration below epitomizes the definition of teamwork.

It was 1970. The New Orleans Saints football team was trailing the Detroit Lions seventeen to sixteen with two seconds remaining. A field goal would win the game, but would have to sail a record sixty-three yards. Tom Dempsey of the Saints made that field goal, resulting in a win for the Saints. This is a record that still stands today, but most impressive was the response by Dempsey. He said, "The thing that I remember most is that *we* won!" Dempsey didn't seek recognition for himself, but rather for his entire team. This was all made even more incredible by the fact that Dempsey had to overcome a major handicap: He was born without a right hand and only half a right foot. This was the foot used to make the record-setting kick!

Each day in our profession we are faced with challenges and choices. We can do things for ourselves, or for our team. We can have a positive attitude with a winning spirit or a negative attitude with a whining spirit. We can complain about our handicap or we can focus on what it takes to have the team win.

Before you can become a better teammate you need to give yourself a litmus test and ask yourself, "How do I deal with the success of my peers?" Are you genuinely happy for them, or do you scoff at their successes only to wish they were yours? Being a good teammate can be difficult because it takes time and time is money. Be willing to go the extra yard and share your good ideas or information with your teammates. Some sales reps withhold beneficial information from others on their team because of the time involved or the concern of being surpassed in the sales standings. Those who don't share are usually selfish or lack self-confidence. Today, information is what it is all about. Share the information you get from the Internet, e-mails, or magazines that you read. No one has the time to comb through all of the material each week, so make it a point to share what you have discovered at your meetings. Sharing the information gleaned from this book would be a great start!

Team players are givers, and givers are happy people. They know that "Whatever comes around goes around." A great deal of good can be accomplished at your company if one is not too careful about who gets the credit. If your sales team makes a "go around" with each other, then TEAM surely will stand for "Together Everyone Achieves More"!

Today's tips:

✓ To lose teammates, brag about yourself.

✓ To gain teammates, brag about others.

✓ Point out the best in others, especially when they are not around.

✓ Ponder how to build others up.

✓ Remember people's names.

✓ Small deeds done for a teammate are better than great deeds planned.

✓ Don't win an argument and lose a teammate.

The success of others is just as important as our own success. We are all part of a team, working toward winning the big prize—the big finish! When your teammate is at their lowest point, you need to be at your highest point for them. When they achieve success, offer those congratulations! Our business is not necessarily to get ahead of others, but to get ahead of ourselves! Compete with yourself—break your own records and improve on yesterday today. An improved team member results in an improved team as the parables on page 30 clearly demonstrate.

RUDY **Says:** Be just as enthusiastic about the successes of your teammates this week as you are about your own.

Teamwork Parables

Parable #1

As each bird flaps its wings, it creates an 'uplift' for the bird following. By flying in a V formation, the whole flock adds 71 percent greater flying range than if each bird flew alone.

Basic Truth – "People who share a common direction and sense of community can get where they are going quicker and easier because they are traveling on the thrust of one another."

Parable #2

Whenever a goose falls out of formation, it suddenly feels the drag and resistance of trying to fly alone and quickly gets back into formation to take advantage of the "lifting power" of the bird immediately in front.

Basic Truth – "If we have as much sense as a goose, we will stay in formation with those who are headed the same way as we are going."

Parable #3

When the lead goose gets tired, it rotates back into the formation and another goose flies point.

Basic Truth – "With people as with geese, it pays to take turns doing the hard tasks."

Parable #4

The geese in formation honk from behind to encourage those up front to keep up their speed.

Basic Truth – "We need to be careful what we say when we honk from behind, making sure that we are encouraging."

Parable #5

Finally, when a goose gets sick or wounded or shot down, two geese drop out of formation and follow it down to help protect it. They stay with that goose until it is either able to fly or until it is dead; then they launch out on their own to catch up with their group.

Basic Truth – "If we have as much sense as the geese, we shall stand by each other like that."

Chapter 5

"I Just Had It; Where Did It Go?"...Organization

ROGET'S *21ST CENTURY THESAURUS* LISTS ONE OF THE definitions of organization to mean "To be responsible for." The sales professional is responsible for organization in all areas of operation, from the calls that have to be made to the unending paperwork that bombards us on a daily basis. When you were young you were the one responsible for cleaning your room, right? (If you answered "no," this could be the underlying reason why you are not organized today!) Today, organizational skills have become more important because of the information overload that is required to keep up with technology. Organization is required not only in your office but in your car, your customer's office, and your home office.

Organization is not to be confused with time management, which is simply making the best use of your time. "Getting organized is an ongoing process, not a destination," states Barbara

Hemphill, author of the *Taming the Paper Tiger* series. Getting organized may seem like a task as large as eating an elephant, but you can accomplish this by taking one bite at a time. The first step is to clean house. *Business Week* gives this advice: "Man's best friend, aside from a dog, is the wastebasket." When the stack of paper on your desk seems to be growing higher by the day, ask yourself this question: "What is the worst thing that could happen if I threw this out? Will someone come looking for it later? Can another copy be obtained from somewhere else?"

The biggest irony in the office automation industry involves how to handle paper. We can explain to a customer the paper path, how it duplexes and then uses the finisher. However, when it comes to taking a simple piece of paper and putting it in its appropriate place, we become disoriented. *The Organized Executive* by Stephanie Winston claims that there are only four and a half things you can do with a piece of paper. (Coming from a background in this industry, you probably are thinking these four and a half things are copy, print, fax, scan, or crumple it and play basketball.) According to Ms. Winston you can:

1. Throw it away
2. Refer to it
3. Act on it
4. File it
5. Read it

To avoid the pitfall of paperwork Hades, you must make a decision every time you acquire a new piece of paper. The key is to handle the piece of paper only *once*. Decide which category it falls into. During the week when I get overloaded I put all incoming new pieces in a red folder in my attaché case that says "File." If I don't have time over my lunch hour to file, I block out at least an hour once per week to go through this file and decide where each piece will ultimately end up.

Digital technology is also changing the way we stay organized not only with paper but in managing your territory effectively. Hand-held Personal Digital Assistants (PDA's) are handy and may be equipped with mini-browsers (for the Internet), built-in voice recorders, and music players. In a sense, they are your electronic card boxes. One advantage it offers is that it's totally portable—it fits in your pocket. The PDA's are far more efficient in keeping you organized than anything else the sales industry has ever had. Not only can they be programmed to tell you when to call but whom as well. Additionally, they will prompt you to the next activity date and allow you to electronically store your weekly/monthly calendar.

There are numerous CRM (Customer Relationship Management) software packages available today such as Act, Gold Mine, and Sales Logic. Some of these will interface with PDA's such as the Palm Pilot to give you all the necessary information you need right in the customer's office. If you really want to get ahead of the game, try setting yourself up with one that will interface to your companies' database management software, such as OMD or LaCrosse, to receive updated service information instantaneously. You'll enjoy not lugging around tons of paper and really appreciate their value when an appointment cancels and you can quickly locate another prospect close by to visit!

If you can't carry around your whole territory electronically yet, you may want to maximize the use of an index card file. Staple business cards acquired during cold calls to an index card or for telephone calls, record the information directly onto the card. Divide the file into sections, categorically referring to the most urgent or promising calls as the "hot" file, thirty days response. I'd recommend making a copy of all of these and having them on you at all times. The other set remains in your card file box at the office. You can't afford to misplace a card and lose a prospect. Also, if it's hot and the prospect calls you while in the field, you'll have the pertinent information at your fingertips, which is always impressive. Detailed notes should also be included on these cards based on discussions you have had with your prospect (or suspect). If you call them on a snowy day and they're headed to Florida for vacation next week and are not in the market for another six months, make a note of it. Call them in four months and mention, "When I spoke with you on February 4 during the snowstorm you mentioned two important events. First, you were headed to Florida and second, you may be looking for office equipment soon..." People are impressed when you follow up with detail and a personal touch. You'll find them more willing to continue the conversation, too, and all because you were organized.

The rest of your card file should be organized into twelve-month sections. As you talk to someone and they give you a time frame, file their information about one to two months prior to that projected time. If they are the proud owner of a brand new machine(s) and won't be in the market for another three years, file a note to contact them in twelve months. Why? Because you shouldn't be thinking like the customer when it comes to office equipment. Your thoughts should be, "What if technology changes even more and they need to assimilate the Internet into their office products? What if they grow and need a second system?" Finally, and my favorite, is, "Oh, oh, did I ask them about a fax?" Many salespersons concentrate too much on copying/printing and miss an easy sale.

Computers are thought of by many as simply an information piece, which they are, but this information must also be organized to enable quick and easy access. Make sure throughout your career that you create folders that will keep you organized through all phases of the sales cycle. When you listen to a tape, read a book, receive training, or share a great idea, record it by subject matter in your computer. Over the course of time you will have excellent information available at your fingertips on how to be one up on the competition. Make sure your computer has organized folders for print samples, cost justifications, and competitive information, to mention a few important characteristics.

Being organized is not a personality characteristic. It is a skill and state of mind anyone can learn. Ask yourself if the objects on your desk, in your briefcase, on the PC, or in the car justify the space they take up. If you notice you have not used them for the last thirty to sixty days, put them in the back of the line and move everything up a notch. If you haven't accessed them in a year—throw them out! A few more practical tips:

- ✓ Have notes to post on your papers that say "Clear out by" or "Throw away by" and give a date.
- ✓ Make sure you stay organized during "low times" of the day. Instead of going out for lunch, eat at your desk while you organize.
- ✓ Make a weekly appointment to organize. Ideal times would be at the beginning or end of each week.
- ✓ Complete one task at a time.

Becoming a master of organization is not difficult—it just takes time and planning. The hardest part is the beginning. Once the system is initiated, the organization develops a flow and you suddenly feel in control. From categorizing the endless papers you find on your desktop to recording and filing important sales information, the result will be your ability to spend more time pursuing sales. Your prospects will be impressed by your ability to recall details which shows them you are attentive to their needs, giving them that appealing personal touch.

RUDY Says: First, clean up now and start all over again no matter how long it takes. Second, organize your work area so if you talk to a prospect you can find anything in seconds *without* having to leave your chair (hope your chair swivels).

Chapter 6

Positively Positive...Attitude

PERHAPS THE MOST BASIC STATE OF MIND NEEDED TO SUC-
ceed in selling involves attitude. How do you portray yourself to
others? How do you respond to them? Attitude is everything in
our profession—it can make or break a sale. The office products
industry is amazing and the world has become a better place
because of us. Major world decisions are made in a matter of seconds because we can copy, fax, scan, and print instantaneously.
Communist leaders can no longer lie and get away with it because
the truth could be faxed or e-mailed into a communist country by
a relative with the real news. Fortune 500 executives can't meet
until the copy machine produces quality copies for their meetings.
Finally, you don't have to miss any of the ball game on television
because you can fax in your pizza order with directions to your
home. Think about it: Every day, all over the country, thousands of
workers are lined up, yes lined up, just to touch a little green
button on one of our machines! Every second, numerous workers
click "file" and "print" and in seconds their projects are complete.

We are wanted, although you would not know it at times the way we are treated.

Some of you are probably thinking, "All right, you went a little overboard on this attitude business—haven't I heard enough of this 'Everything is rosy' and 'Be positive' stuff?" I can respond to this with a solid and sincere *"No, you haven't."* Furthermore, if this describes your present attitude, you definitely need to read on.

Attitude is difficult to define because what may be good for one may be not so good for another. It's more about perception. The key here is to make sure that those around you perceive you as someone whose glass is half full, not half empty. This makes you an enjoyable person, which in turn will make those around you want to listen to you, to spend more time with you. This is the all-important beginning of a successful relationship. Basically, you control your attitude or it controls you. You wake up and invent yourself for the day—you create the world you live in—every single day.

Napoleon Hill stated, "Whatever your mind can conceive, it can believe, and then you can achieve." Again, this puts you in the driver's seat. The first step involved in an attitude "check-up from the neck-up" in your office products career is to make certain that you believe in your product, service, and company. If the attitude generated from these factors cannot be that of a positive nature, you need to ask yourself if you are in the right industry. Second, analyze your work habits because there may be obstacles that alter your attitude. Some common bad habits may include disorganization, a lack of effort, managing time ineffectively, or just not having the experience to utilize the sales skills necessary to succeed. Fortunately, all of these areas can be improved to make you a more productive salesperson.

Attitude also means having the correct balance in your life. Just like a bicycle needs many spokes to function properly, you too must have the various "spokes" to help balance your work life. It's all a matter of proportion. Life is not all work. What other activities "fill you up"? How about time with your family, friendships, or involvement with other worthwhile community activities? By creating many facets to your life, those that are fulfilling, you will be a happier and more positive person. Just as important, if one of your "spokes" fails you still have the others to keep you going. If you live to work and work deteriorates for a month, you may end up in a long attitude slump.

Attitude is a matter of perception, or perspective. Sometimes difficulties can arise because as we look around it seems as though everyone has the shinier, more updated model. Yet, we are so blessed to be living in this country, so blessed that our visions become distorted. We become down on ourselves after watching our television sets—witnessing first hand the luxuries and successes this country has to offer. Some years ago, a friend of mine, John Engle, gave up his successful career in the office automation industry to become a missionary in Haiti with Beyond Borders. The newsletters that I receive from him really give me a reality check. Talk about putting our lives into perspective! The average *annual* income for the citizens of Haiti is less than $125.00! Some people spend that amount for one dinner out!

Your behavior breeds the behavior of those around you. Think about it. How do you respond when confronted with a negative person? Have you ever noticed that if your reaction is positive and concerned, you can turn this person's mood around? Mimic that person's glum mood and I can guarantee that you will get nowhere. Your sensitivity in this situation will help you to steer the meeting to a more upbeat mood, thus creating the atmosphere for a successful conversation. Start today with enthusiasm. The last four letters of enthusiasm are "IASM," which can stand for "I am sold myself." With this tool your attitude has to be positive. When you believe in something and you know that you can provide a great service for a customer, it really shows. There is something contagious about someone who believes in themselves, their service, or product. I enjoy the professionals who can illuminate a room with their presence because of their positive vibes. I also feel guilty at times when I am confronted with someone who is very positive. It forces me to not only look at my attitude at that exact point in time but to make a quick adjustment for the better.

Jeff Johnson, who has been a very successful salesman and manager for over ten years in the Chicago market, had this advice to share on attitude: "The key is to start the week off on Monday with something fun to look forward to. Schedule a breakfast, lunch, or an appointment with a key account to set the stage for the entire week with a great attitude."

If Monday starts and nothing is set up, you may have to begin your week with cold calls. Prospecting is vital to the success of any sales professional, but if it's not planned and becomes a last minute desperation measure just to have something to do, it could lead to a bad attitude.

Speaking of prospecting and attitude, the following story sums it all up: Two competing copier salespersons needed a new challenge so they were both sent to a new territory far from their cozy office. After two weeks one of them called back to his boss and said, "Boss, it is incredible out here, no one has a copier, get me out of here!" The second salesperson worked two weeks also and called back to his boss and said, "Boss, it is incredible out here, no one has a copier, send me all the inventory you have immediately!"

"Look at life through the windshield, not the rear-view mirror," suggests Byrd Baggett from *The Book of Excellence*. When can you begin? Right now—with the right attitude!

Yiddish folk tale

An
old
man sat
outside the walls
of a great city. When
travelers approached, they
would ask him, "What kind of
people live here?" And the old
man would answer, "What kind of people
lived in the place where you came from?"
If the travelers answered "Only bad people
lived in the place where we came from" then
the old man would reply "Continue on; you will
find only bad people here." But if the travelers
answered "Only good people lived in the place where
we came from" then the old man would say, "Enter, for here,
too, you will find only good people."

RUDY Says: You can't always control what happens to you, but you can control how you respond. Encouragement is food for the heart and hearts are always hungry. When you see someone who is "hungry," feed him or her!

Understand

To understand your job is quite simple—it is to close sales. In one day of work you can learn what the primary steps of the sales cycle include. However, it will take years to truly understand how to effectively use them. Basically, the customer dictates how they should be sold. The salesperson needs to understand that changes in technology will lead to changes in how the sales cycle is utilized. Knowing the sales cycle is just half the battle. Your execution and persistence are mandatory to "bring the orders in!"

Chapter 7

Telemarketing

GOOD TELEPHONE SKILLS ARE VITAL TO A SUCCESSFUL career in the office products sales profession. From the pre-call planning and delivery of the call to leaving a voice mail message, how you handle this important sales tool can have a great impact on your success.

I dislike the term "telemarketing" because "tel" triggers the meaning "to tell" in my mind. The confusion in sales is that telling is *not* selling. Many salespersons make a telephone call and immediately start talking (telling) too much. Maybe we should refer to these calls as "Sellution-marketing" calls. The goal of the call is to do a little "investigation" into finding problems for which we can provide that valuable solution. This is how we discover that all-important "need," which leads to the appointment, demonstration, and close.

The initial twenty seconds are the most critical in delivering your message to the prospect. When the telephone is answered the person is wondering:

Why is this person calling me?

How long will this call take?

What is in it for me?

Provide the answer for all three of these questions immediately! Most of the time a person will listen if you create an interest or give a benefit statement. A statement such as "Digital technology is vastly improving the paper flow of many businesses today. I'd like to share some ideas with you on how my company may possibly help." This statement is simple and offers a benefit without even mentioning a product.

When you plan what you will be communicating on the telephone, write the words as an outline, not a script. No one wants to listen to someone with a "canned" pitch. Then, break down what you will be saying to evaluate its effectiveness. For example, after introducing yourself it is common to ask, "How are you doing?" Instantly, the receiver may be thinking, "Oh no, here come a sales pitch." Try using positive statements such as "I hope your day is going well," and then listen to the response. Your next statement can be something along the lines of, "This call should take only about a minute." This allows the receiver to drop their guard and think, "Good, I won't be stuck on the telephone for five to ten minutes but I can spare a minute."

Another way to lower the guard during the introduction is to state, "I'm calling because I haven't helped your company in the past and I'm not sure if I can now." Continue with, "I'm confident that with all of the technology changes recently we can find a way to improve your productivity (or costs)." Don't forget that it is not just what you say, but *how* you say it—remember the VIPS from Chapter 3!

It is important that you come across as believable. To be believable, you must show that you are fully knowledgeable about the product you are attempting to sell, that you possess a positive attitude, that you use interesting voice inflection, and that you are professional. Practice the message you want to get across, and how you will say it. Ask yourself, "If I were listening to me, would I buy from this person?" Tape-record yourself. Does it sound like you are trying to sell a product or solve a problem? When you listen to the recording, are you yourself convinced?

Listening skills have an important role in the telephone call. You will experience a short, one-sided conversation if all you do is bust through with your pitch. Stop talking when you feel the prospect is about to say something and listen to what is important to them. An objection may be brought up, which would give you the opportunity to provide a solution. More interest is now created, which leads to a continued conversation. Be careful not to relay your disappointment at the mention of the first objection...always be positive. Use your enthusiasm to bring the conversation back around.

Pre-call planning is vital to a productive day of "Sellution-marketing" calling. Some strategies to consider:

- ✓ Clean your desk. Make sure you have all the materials you will need to make your presentation smooth, professional, and upbeat.

- ✓ Clear your mind. Concentrate on what you are going to say and *how* you are going to say it.

- ✓ Plan your call. Each call should have a definite objective.

- ✓ Try different approaches until you become more effective with the presentation of your message. You will be able to determine which you're more comfortable with. Be consistent in maintaining a uniform approach to increase the effectiveness of your calls.

- ✓ Develop a rhythm. Set a block of one to two hours and call thirty to forty prospects in a row. Another method is to set a goal of, for example, fifteen calls. When you finish these fifteen you allow yourself a short break. If you don't set a target, it can become too easy to give up.

✓ Don't spend more than one minute between calls. More calls result in more sales!

✓ When you begin your calling, make a notation of the start time. After completion of your calls, note the time that you ended. You may find a pattern developing in the time of day that you are most productive. (Early or late morning, afternoon, etc.)

✓ Don't allow yourself to be put on hold for long periods of time. If you're on hold for more than one minute, just hang up and try again.

✓ Stay positive! Your product isn't for everyone immediately so don't let a negative response get you down!

Voice mail has made it more difficult to reach the correct person. It can take three to four dialing attempts to reach the desired party. An effective strategy with voice mail is to leave only your first name and telephone number. This is captivating to some in that their attention turns to curiosity about who you are and why you are calling. Business people are often curious and don't want to miss out on a call that may be profitable to them. (Warning! You must keep good call records so that when the calls are returned by these curiosity seekers, the information is directly at your fingertips and you won't be caught off guard.) To respond with confidence helps assure the contact that you know what you are doing, which in turn makes them confident that they could count on you and what you are trying to sell them.

Sometimes calls that are sent to voice mail can be rerouted to the operator by pressing "0" (zero). This will allow for contact with a "real person" at which time you can ask for the desired contact party's extension. This is extremely effective because the next time you dial, you can enter this extension and increase your chances of getting through. Use this voice mail strategy to avoid ending up in voice "jail."

Another strategy for voice mail is to request that you be connected through to the sales department if you have trouble getting through the "deceptionist." There are two ways to handle the sales department, depending on your personality. First, state that you, too, are a salesperson and would like the decision-maker's name. Second, you could try the "Oops, I was looking for purchasing and...could you help me with their names so that I can be more professional when I speak with them?"

Leave your message on voice mail if there is no answer. After all, you did spend the time gathering all of the pertinent information to initiate the call. You might as well finish the job with the message, because no goals will be scored if you don't at least take a shot.

Let's not forget the message you record on your own voice mail. Always leave a *short* but positive and enthusiastic message such as, "Good decision calling ABC" or "I'm glad you called ABC. Leave a message and I'll get back with you soon to tell you why!"

No one wants to take forty-five seconds to listen to your message explaining your daily schedule and why you can't answer the telephone immediately. Make your message unique and positive to differentiate you from the competition.

The use of the telephone is such a vital part of our sales profession. How we choose to utilize this tool will make a huge difference in the success of our career. Keep in mind that when you call, most people are busy and only about twenty percent will see you as contributing to their bottom line. Make sure they know you won't be long and that you are there to help them—you want to set up the appointment that will prove to them how. One more thought...let's not forget what was used so effectively in years past–a little respect and gratitude. Many executives and pur-chasers have been in the business world for quite a while and appreciate such phrases as "Do you have a minute" or "Is now a good time to talk?"

RUDY **Says:** Smile and dial. Make sure it sounds like you are either trying to contribute to their bottom line or trying to solve a problem and not just trying to sell something. Practice by tape recording yourself and check your pace, tone, and voice inflec-tion.

Chapter 8

Cold Calling

IMAGINE THAT YOU ARE SITTING POOLSIDE ON A SULTRY summer day. After a while the heat becomes unbearable so you decide to plunge into the cool water. Initially your body experiences a cool shock, but you soon adjust to the new temperature and experience true enjoyment.

Similarly, cold calling is about being uncomfortable (for most of us) and then taking the "plunge" into your territory. Soon the idea of making these calls is not so agonizing. It is after you master this that you can replace the "C" in cold with a "G"–to make the gold!

Cold calling, without a doubt, is one of the most difficult components of your sales career, but it also must be mastered because it is so important. Your presentation, preparation, and attitude will always play an integral role but some adjustments will have to be made when technologies change.

A few years ago the philosophy went something like, "Don't fight gravity, start high." It was common to try to reach the highest in command and be directed to the individual responsible for purchasing office equipment. Now, due to the changes and advancement in technology, the highest in command probably isn't aware of the needs and applications warranted. There could be someone in the communications (telephone) department in charge of Internet and facsimile purchases. The Information Technology (IT) department may have certain employees assigned to the management of network connections. The graphics department may want to evaluate the color quality and scanning capability. Factor into these the possibility that somewhere in the middle of all these positions lies a traditional office manager or purchaser who must also be appealed to.

To view this in a more positive light, just consider your territory to have grown! This allows you more chances to find a good prospect with every call. Every business requires some level of office equipment, which is the beauty of this industry. On average, the typical copier, fax, or printer is replaced every four to five years. Even a small office today can have three to five pieces of equipment which means each year there is a good possibility of at least one piece being replaced or upgraded. This alone should generate enough motivation to get your prospecting in high gear. Make the contacts before someone else beats you to it! The good news is that once you've sold the initial connected machine, you'll be contacted first for those needed in the future.

Preparation is definitely the key for cold calling, and this doesn't mean loading yourself up with brochures and flyers. Days and times need to be set aside for these calls, which allow you to prepare yourself mentally. If you don't schedule time for this in advance, it will be too easy to find something more comfortable to accomplish. Because of the rejection factor, it is difficult to schedule an entire day for cold calling so break your calls into time frames and selections. Make a particular number of calls to new prospects, then some to referrals, and finally finish with calls to previously contacted businesses.

The use of cold calling has a major impact in the yearly financial rewards you are striving to achieve. Once you set a dollar level, determine how many prospecting calls will be needed to generate the revenue goal you've set. After the first month on the job your objective should be about eighty cold calls and eighty telephone calls per week. Eventually this will lead to ten to twelve appointments that will turn into three to four demonstrations per week. Ultimately, you should be closing one to one and a half deals per week. As you gain more experience, the digital products you demonstrate and close will be the higher-end products, leading to more commissions. Once you establish yourself, you may find that time for prospecting calls is diminishing, but beware! Make sure you cold call consistently to keep yourself "lean and mean." Many sales reps who tend to shy away from them after a while start to become "soft" and business drops off a few months later.

When initiating a cold call, your most likely first encounter will be with the receptionist. When I was first trained in copier sales in 1984, it was taught that receptionists (also referred to as deceptionists) were the enemy and I was therefore trained in strategies to maneuver around them. A few years later, when the electronic typewriter boom was in full swing, most salespersons realized that the person residing in this position was actually their friend! They were very involved in the purchasing decision with at least one of your many products. Taking this into consideration, make certain that the first few words are not only warm, but give a benefit statement suitable for the receptionist.

Keep it simple. After introducing yourself, state, "I'd like to be of some help to your company. Could you help me by first letting me know whom I would set up an appointment with to introduce the benefits of digital technology?" Notice this introduction was short, polite, and you asked for their help. You were not demanding or pressuring and you asked to set up an appointment. Each company will be different and you must be able to read and adapt to their environment. If the receptionist appears to be busy, be sure to acknowledge this by saying, "It looks like you are very busy, but may I ask your help for about thirty seconds?" A more witty comment would be, "You are very busy and this is why I stopped by!" Then, introduce yourself immediately and provide a benefit statement that your product will make their office work easier and more efficient.

If, upon your arrival, you are screened as to what your product line concerns, you can keep it vague and state, "Network issues, digital printing, computer faxing, and scanning." Then, inquire as to how many people are involved in these issues, because more than one appointment may be needed. You've just given the receptionist the alternative close and the answer may come out before he or she forgets they were initially going to screen you. It's vital to every call that you listen to responses or objections and handle them before you continue.

Two major mistakes can be improved upon overnight. First, talk the language of the receptionist. You may want to incorporate words similar to "easier," "relaxing," or "fun" when giving a benefit statement. Receptionists are not impressed with phrases like "more productive," "saving money," or "return on investment." Save language such as this for the "bottom-line" person. Second, a red flag is raised when you introduce yourself only to immediately spout, "Who's in charge of purchasing office equipment?" Reaching this person is the ultimate goal, but the perception of the receptionist is that you are a pushy salesperson who has no respect for their position. Show interest and courtesy at all times and remember that listening is the highest form of courtesy. If all goes well, don't be surprised if the receptionist can set up the appointment for you. Don't be afraid to ask if the person is available for a few minutes on the spot—why save it for a telephone call if you can begin immediately? If you are able to meet with the prospect at short notice, introduce yourself, show gratitude, and give your benefit statement. Ask if you can sit down because, in my experience, I've found that if the appointment progresses with you standing up, it will be short and without genuine interest.

Cold calling can wear and tear on you so try to partner up once in a while with an experienced rep at your office. Just like when you exercise, it's easier to stay motivated when someone is with you. Also, the most effective prospecting involves your current customers, though this is often overlooked. Ask satisfied customers if they know of anyone in the market for office products, or if they have a need for more! Believe it or not, all of your customers are not loyal and they may not bring their need to your attention unless you ask. They may not know you offer computer or Internet faxing because in the past you only discussed their copying and printing needs. Don't forget to prospect for accessories involving items you've sold them in the past, either. Normally there isn't any competition and the sale tends to be more profitable.

That swimming pool mentioned earlier—make enough cold calls and it's yours! Financial rewards will come if you just make the calls, prepare in advance, and have a true interest in every individual and business you meet up with. The reality is that when cold calling, you will experience individuals who treat you poorly, but this may be indicative of their low self-esteem or meager professionalism. Be better than this, because after all, your job is to look for the "goldness"...not the coldness!

RUDY **Says:** Turn the cold call into a gold call. Treat everyone you meet like they are the decision maker. Make sure you smile and walk another mile!

Chapter 9

Qualifying

When dining out, have you ever ordered dessert despite the fact that you were full? Perhaps what enticed you were the emotions that overcame you as the dessert tray was presented. When surveying the delectable contents of the tray, your affection for sweet endings began to take over, telling your stomach that it could access that portion designated to desserts even though the main stomach had reached its capacity. The mind (facts) voted "no," but the soul (emotions) voted "yes."

Effective qualifying is essentially the same, because both factual and emotional questions are utilized together to gain a genuine interest in the solution that you can potentially provide. If all purchases were made solely upon the facts presented (features and price), selling office products would be quite boring and not nearly as profitable.

Qualifying is the process of asking the right questions during an appointment with the prospect to determine if there is a need for the office equipment you are selling. Qualifying becomes less frustrating if you are able to realize the buyer's mentality and prepare yourself with the proper mindset and questions. A general understanding of the buyer's position can definitely foster a successful relationship, which leads to your success during the sales cycle. Enthusiasm, conviction, and gratitude play an important role here, because a prospect may not understand all the network connections and digital features but they can definitely comprehend the transference of your feelings. Perhaps the chief frustration involved in qualifying is the old "status quo." Plain and simple, the fear of the unknown, or reluctance to change, will definitely become an obstacle in your efforts to secure a sale. Keep in mind that the prospect's job many times is to conceal and not reveal all of the pertinent information. During the appointment you may encounter statements such as "Service is great" or "The current product meets all of my needs." There is the possibility that customers may not be telling the truth in order to protect themselves or to end the appointment because they have an important meeting or a hot date!

Prior to each appointment you need to determine your objective. Is it to get more information, find a contact name, schedule a demonstration, deliver pricing, or all of the above? The questions you ask should revolve around your quest. Just as important is to make certain you are meeting with the appropriate person. Just because an appointment agreed to meet with you doesn't mean they can buy from you. Don't ask them, "Are you the right person?" because their answer may be "Yes" (and may be only partly correct) or because they may become defensive.

Instead, phrase your question like this: "The last time you bought, what was the *process*?" Or "If you decide to invest in my digital system, what is the procedure for acquiring it?" A better way of saying "Who besides yourself is responsible...?" is "I understand this is an important decision for your company. Whom would you like to involve besides yourself in this decision?" From the responses given you can deduce whether or not you are on the right track.

Typically, your company has a list of helpful questions to assist you in fact finding. Some examples: 1. When is your lease ending? 2. How many prints and copies per month are you presently doing? 3. What type of network are you currently using?

These factual questions are close-ended, meaning they require only a few words of response. Make sure that you include questions that are open-ended as well because they require more thought and dialogue from the prospect. The question mentioned earlier in regard to the "buying process" is a good example of a question that requires the prospect to "open up."

To succeed with the prospect, though, you need to develop a list of questions that involve the emotions (feelings) of not only the subject but the person as well. When my brother Kyle was purchasing product for a Chicago sign company, I asked him what enticed him to buy. I'll never forget his response. His response was, "Whoever talks about my son, Zach... That's the person who will get my order!" He lives the old philosophy of "People don't care about how much you know until they know how much you care!" This means that you can have an excellent product with outstanding pricing but without the proper emotional questions and concerns of the buyer, you'll not succeed! When entering the office of a new appointment, scrutinize the environment. Is the desk messy...are there awards hanging on the wall...are there family pictures scattered about? Many sales people have commented that they stay away from such personalization because they are afraid their interest will be misconstrued, risking the chance of sounding phony. How true—if your interest is not genuine. My point is, we should all take a genuine interest in others, because if our interest lies solely in the finality of the sale, we *will* come across as fakes!

Emotional questions involve nudging prospects to ponder their lives outside of their work boundaries. Let's say that during an appointment you explain to a prospect how one hour per day could be saved. You can appeal to the buyer emotionally by directing this time savings into his personal time account—pointing out that this additional hour gained could be spent finishing up that other project which would allow him to finally get home for dinner on time, work on that golf game, or spend more time coaching his children's soccer team! Emotional questions are powerful and allow you to build a rapport, confidence, and trust. They are also career builders that allow you to develop friendships and a loyal customer base.

Your effective emotional questioning requires practice. Write down the questions ahead of time. A simple close-ended question could be, "How long have you been purchasing office equipment?" The answer requires a one or two word fact. To appeal more to the emotions of the buyer, ask, "What do you like (or dislike) most about buying office equipment and why?" You can determine from the response a good sense of direction for the remainder of the appointment.

If the buyer is new to the position, you may need to spend more time educating him or her. If the buyer is a veteran, you should "speed up" the process. Sometimes the experienced buyer is well aware of how they want the buying cycle to continue. Make sure you load up with fun questions during the appointment, that you add some spice to the typical qualifying questions. Some amazingly easy questions (and they grab attention) are, "How do you like to be sold?" and "Are you the least expensive in your industry?" and "Would it help gain approval if I created a spreadsheet of justifications?" and "What can I do to earn *all* of your business?" The likelihood of getting all the correct information is next to nil, but it could quite possibly open a whole new avenue of information involving the purchasing past (why and where did they make the purchase).

Qualifying involves a lot of strategy and thinking. Five guidelines to consider during the appointment are:

1. When someone is buying an office product there are basically six criteria they will weigh out: Quality of print/copy, productivity, reliability, versatility, convenience, and economy (price). Make sure you find out which ones are the most important.

2. Compliment the prospect on a good question or important concern they have.

3. Don't explain your product with your jargon. Acronyms such as ADF (Automatic Document Feeder), APS (Automatic Paper Selection), and CCD (Charged Coupled Device) may be second nature to us but you may lose the decision maker.

4. Instead of inquiring as to what features they are looking for, ask about the documents they are copying, printing, or faxing. Ask to see them and then explain how your system can accommodate them.

5. Use a sight seller and color in your presentation because key points will be more memorable. The use of samples enhances your explanation of digital features.

Make use of the buyer's emotions when qualifying an appointment. We are all members of the human race and appreciate being understood as well as interested in—this is the way we were created. Use this to your advantage, as a successful sales career is heavily reliant upon relationships. Emotional questioning does require practice, as well as some keen observations. Mastering these types of questions along with the factual ones will be beneficial in qualifying and setting the tone for your visit. Your presentation of the "dessert tray" during the qualifying process will indeed play upon those hidden emotions of the buyer.

Who says you can't have your cake and eat it too?

RUDY **Says:** Make a list of qualifying questions that will involve the emotions of the person communicating with you. The right questions will lead to the right answers, which will lead to the right solutions and finally the sale!

Chapter 10

Objections

"I'M NOT INTERESTED." "WE'RE NOT IN THE MARKET." "I'LL think it over!"

"Objections Training" used to be one of the easiest segments to cover. I remember an assignment given in college pertaining to the sales environment in which I chose the topic of handling objections. I found a plethora of information on the subject. My dad, who has been selling for over forty-five years, had quite an encyclopedia of information with one-line, appropriate responses.

In any event, it used to be "Find the prospect, appease their objections, and close them." I can remember it being said that a sales call didn't even begin until the prospect said a wholehearted "No."

It seemed so simple then. Soon, overcoming objections went to the other extreme, which made it a complicated process. I studied flowcharts that examined six steps and went something like this: Listen, question to qualify, emphasize, confirm and isolate, answer the concern, then ask for the order.

The research I've completed shows that the 1950s–'70s consisted of one-liners, the '80s–'90s tackled the whole process, and the late '90s–'00s...well, it's much more involved and quite challenging! But this is all okay, because as members of the sales profession, it is what we enjoy and is what keeps us going strong.

Buyers seem to become more educated every year, which means objections need to be handled with care. Prospects don't appreciate a long-winded response or to be closed after every objection. They want someone who is in a more consultative role who will comprehend what it is they are looking for and then give their recommendation. Witty responses can no longer overcome objections. Instead, a true understanding of the situation is needed. If the objection is answered too quickly and is "canned," the prospect will lose confidence in you. The best way to avoid this and to assure an accurate response is to *restate what you interpreted the customer to say*. This will enhance the understanding. During your restatement, it also buys you time to devise an appropriate response, all the while showing that you are listening to the message they are trying to convey.

Objections can occur during every stage of the sales cycle: Prospecting, qualifying, demonstrating, and closing. The difficulty lies within deciding the reason for the objection. It is easiest to tackle an objection when directly in front of the customer. In this position, you are pretty certain that a decision must be made. The objective reasoning here is usually pressure related. The decision must be made, and the prospect wants to be certain that it will be a good one. What they are really looking for here is the reassurance that you can provide the best product, deal, and service they could possibly find. (I like to categorize these types of objections as "real" objections.)

Other objections may not be so "real." Telephones are the most common environment for these. These objections are utilized for nothing other than to provide an abrupt end to your conversation. However, these objections can also provide you with vital sales strategy information. Many times these are actual buying criteria, so give them your full attention.

The objections have now been presented. What demeanor should be used and how should you respond? Answer an objection with care. It is best to be slow to answer (pause three to four seconds) or to even respond with a question. If the question comes up, "How well does your office equipment perform in a dusty environment?" you should reply, "Tell me more about your concern with dusty conditions." Find out specifics. Use your investigative skills to determine the background of the customer's quest for a new product—the entire story from the beginning. It's interesting how, when phrased appropriately, information can be gained without being direct. You appear to be the expert consultant while leaving the competing salesperson (pardon the pun) in the dust!

How you strategically react to an objection can make or break the sale. For example, if a prospect believes that your product does not perform functions that are necessary to his company and application, the most typical response would be of a direct "Yes, it can" nature. Rather than retorting immediately, respond with an investigative question along the lines of, "That's an interesting statement; where did you hear that?" at which time the prospect will probably state the source (ABC competitor). This leads to the discovery of your competition! At this point, maximize your strengths along with the competitor's weaknesses.

While prospecting, one of the problems most often encountered involves time, as in "I have no time to talk with you." A great response to this objection is an appropriate, "That's why I am calling! With the changes in office technology today I am sure I can save you additional time in your work day."

Then there is the "No money available" objection to which you can respond, "That's why I want to discuss our equipment in more detail. I can provide a proposal that will include a plan to save you money." This art of turning around why the prospect can't do something to making it the reason they should is simple. You simply must first resist the urge to want to give an immediate response back.

Oftentimes, an objection is not always an objection. It may be a cry for more information or justification. Serious buyers want that reassurance and may probe you just to make certain that they are heading in the right direction.

A good litmus test for handling objections is to ask yourself, "Are my responses moving the sale forward?" If not, you may not have uncovered the real objections of your prospect. At this time you have nothing to lose, so make a strong statement, such as, "I feel that I'm not making the necessary progress in trying to help you out. Is there something else I need to know about?" Sincerity and politeness are essential here.

Objections are the necessary evil in the sales environment. They have a purpose and, when handled correctly, lead to the success of the sale. Have some fun with them and use them as a tool, not an obstacle, to win the deal. Change your thinking today and encourage objections. If you don't encounter them regularly, you are not in the game!

RUDY Says: Prospects are all different—one may state a need as a need and another may state a need as an objection. Normally, more objections mean a hunger for more good information. Make sure you handle the objection so you don't get the rejection!

Chapter 11

Demonstrations

Prospecting, appointments, and qualifying are done with the purpose of generating a need for your product. If done correctly, the fun should start with multiple demonstrations each and every week! A good demonstration requires a lot of practice not only on the buttons of your product and tabs on the print driver, but on your creative thinking and professionalism as well.

All demonstrations are not alike. The mood and how the demonstration flows depends upon the needs of the prospect, the product being demonstrated, and the personality of the "audience." Make sure to control the pace as well as any interruptions that may occur. The digital era has definitely changed the way we demonstrate. The first determination you have to make is if your demonstration will be as a connected or stand-alone product. If it is connected, find out what the primary use will be: Walk-up or from the computer workstation. If it will be from the workstation (or your laptop), it is important to demonstrate as close as you can to the product in order to monitor and "show off" the performance and power. As far as what to start demonstrating first, the connected or stand-alone, ask your prospect!

Stand-Alone Demonstration:

There are numerous ways to proceed with a demonstration, but the following nine steps give you a strong foundation to follow:

1. **Introduction:** Introduce or reintroduce yourself and the company you are representing. It is crucial to remember the name of everyone attending the demonstration. This is the time to relay your excitement, enthusiasm, and energy!

2. **Overview manufacturer:** Give a brief overview (approximately one minute) of the manufacturer and why it would be a good decision to purchase their product. What unique advantages or support as a company do they offer, and how will they benefit the prospect?

3. **Review needs:** Review the prospect's needs (usually three to four primary ones) and ask if there have been any changes to this list. Include any additions in the demonstration, but add them onto the end. Don't answer them immediately. Stick to the original sequence.

4. **Intention to advance:** This step is vital! Ironically, this is the step that is left out most often. You must gain a commitment that if the demonstration goes well then you can advance to the final step, which is closing. This step has also been referred to as a "Pre-Commitment" or "Trial Close." Basically, you are saying, "If this product meets all of your needs perfectly today, are you in the position to fill out the paperwork?"

   Of course, don't use that wording because it is too strong and old-fashioned today. A more toned-down version would be, "Once you see how perfectly this product meets your needs, when would you like it delivered?" Make sure you develop a statement that is comfortable to you that also portrays an energetic yet serious tone. Even if you met two weeks ago and found out the answer, ask it again because a lot can change in two weeks. The closing portion will definitely be much easier when you refer back to the commitment you gain here.

5. **Start demonstration:** At this time, there are three different directions to take:

   (a) Give an overview of the product to get your audience comfortable. It may seem second nature to you, but may be intimidating to them. Show the design and layout such as locations of the paper drawers, finisher and document feeder. Then, proceed to Step 6.

   (b) Start with the fireworks! Show something flashy or unique first to gain their attention and to get them excited. If the group you are demonstrating to has that "impatient" look, don't lose their attention by being stale and slow. Then, proceed to Step 6.

   (c) The prospect has already presented a list of needs. Identify that first need and demonstrate the efficiency of your product in satisfying this requirement. Make sure you gain the commitment. Step 6 is the continuation of the rest of the needs.

6. **Identify each need and gain commitment:** One by one, address the prospect's list of needs while gaining the commitment that what you have demonstrated will, in fact, meet all of those needs.

7. **Summarize all steps:** When all needs and commitments have been met, summarize the demonstration and then ask, "Did you think of any other needs during the demonstration or do you have any questions?" You don't want any surprises when you try to close the deal.

8. **Grand finale:** Usually this is the point at which the sales-

person closes-after all, needs have been discussed and you have demonstrated how your product will be able to meet these needs. You have worked hard to get to this point and since you have center stage, it's time for the grand finale! By now you should have been getting the prospects to say "yes" a lot (or at least have their heads nodding in an approving manner). Now is your chance to add one more plug as to why you are the best choice. This is your opportunity to provide the prospect with that service that surpasses that of the competition! Perhaps it's the personal service that you will follow through with, your company's reputation *after* the sale, or anything that differentiates you from the competition. This step is very effective if you believe in your product, company, and self.

9. **Close:** This is the most rewarding and enjoyable step. Refer back to the "Intention to advance" (Step 4) for the closing statement. If you have followed the above steps correctly and professionally, a successful close is inevitable!

Connected Demonstration:

The connected demonstration will vary depending on whom you are demonstrating to. Everyone needs to see the features that are included with the driver and what's under the "Properties" button. If the IT department is involved it is imperative that you also show them the network management tools. Many controllers, printer boards, or Raster Image Processors (RIPs) come equipped with administration tools to monitor printers on the network. Some are equipped to use the web-based browser on your desktop operating system to monitor and control network traffic. The IT department needs to be assured your system setup will run seamlessly with what they are using.

It is very important that your prospect(s) can sit in front of the monitor or laptop screen for the best view. You may have to sit on either side slightly but make sure you control the mouse because you know exactly where to click. Be careful not to move the cursor around too fast! You know where you're clicking but no one else does and following the cursor could give a dizzying/nauseating feeling.

"Demonstration kits" with originals aren't needed (unless scanning is involved), but you will need a file folder with various documents to print out. The easiest way is to store it on the computer Desktop and label it simply "Demonstrations." Have a variety of files ready to print out from basic Word documents to graphic-heavy PDF files. The last thing a prospect wants to see is you moving the cursor all over to find a decent looking document to print that's not too personal. Make sure you include multiple page documents to show the simplicity of duplexing and finishing.

Steps 1–4: Basically, the first four steps mentioned in the stand-alone demonstration are the same in the connected demonstration. With Step 2 you may want to add more about the history and success of your digital products and how connectivity is supported.

Steps 5-7: Again, the steps are essentially the same but start with an overview of the print driver. After clicking on "File" and "Print," go to the "Properties" button and click on it to display and explain all of the tabs. Concentrate on their specific applications and needs to gain agreement. After you've finished meeting all of their needs, it's all right to turn over the mouse and let them click around through the various "Tabs" to become comfortable with the layout. This also gives you the opportunity to judge their skill level while they become excited with a more productive way to make it through their workday. If the IT department is included in this portion of the demonstration, go over the networking capabilities to gain their approval. Even if they are not involved at this time it's still nice to show some of the administrative tools to the office personnel. The most important one is to show them where to look to see if their job has printed prior to walking over to the digital system to pick it up.

Steps 8–9: Step 8 may have to be more "digitalized" as far as an impact statement is concerned. Step 9, closing, may not be appropriate at this time because you'll probably have to take them over to your product. The process will probably be an overview of the physical equipment, including the paper path and "insides" of the system. You may also want to put an emphasis on the features that fulfilled their original needs (steps 5-7). However, depending on the situation and response, closing may be just the ticket!

The digital demonstration will take more time but the end result is a higher dollar sale. It is imperative that the demonstration flows smoothly from step to step. Have fun! Remember, it is not only what you say, but also how you say it! People are not necessarily going to buy based on what they hear from you, but based on what they *believe* from you. Your words may go unremembered, but your excitement, professionalism, and smooth demonstration technique will be remembered. Sometimes we forget just how exciting it can be for a prospect to obtain new office equipment! Your initial contact with them may have felt somewhat uneasy, but once they have seen just how beneficial this new piece of equipment will be for them, they become excited! Don't let them down.

RUDY Says: Practice the nine steps of the demonstration extensively until it appears to be one smooth step. Be organized, creative, and don't forget Step 4!

Demonstration Guidelines

The goal of your demonstration is to leave the prospect not with a feeling of "good demonstration" but with the strong desire to purchase your product.

Stand-Alone/Connected	Corresponding Tips
1. Introduction	1. Remember names, relay excitement, have energy
2. Overview manufacturer	2. Why it is a good decision
3. Review needs	3. Don't want any surprises
4. Intention to advance	4. Vital for closing
5. Start demonstration • Overview • Fireworks • Need & commitment	5. Three Ways to start demo • Machine layout • Flashy or unique • Prospect must commit
6. Identify each need and gain commitment	6. One by one, slowly, but surely
7. Summarize all steps	7. Make sure you don't miss anything
8. Grand finale	8. Last chance to impress
9. Close	9. Commission time

❏ Did I do anything creative?

"If the prospect is going to buy a $20,000 system, give them a $20,000 demonstration."

BERNIE LANGERAK, 30-YEAR VETERAN

Chapter 12

Closing

Selling used to have a golden rule that basically stated, "Close, close, close, close, close, and close." Close at least six times during the sales process with each prospect if you want to be a top performer. Indeed the ABC's of closing were "Always Be Closing—close early and close often." But, yesterday's ABC's will get you today's DEF's (Definitely Eliminated From the chance to secure the deal). Today's prospects are much more educated about products and selling techniques and won't allow the pressure tactics of yester-year to persuade their decision-making process. Since the selling style of office products has changed to the "solutions provider" concept, the six-time close is no longer appropriate or appreciated. If your "sales presentation" necessitates more than a few moderately hard closes, you are falling way short on the job because your message is not getting across.

There are two main reasons to close. First, the prospect agrees they have a need (problem) and you can provide the solution. Second, the prospect doesn't necessarily have a problem, but you have the better mousetrap—a more valuable alternative. Sales of digital products are invigorating because they replace machines that aren't necessarily worn out; they simply are not capable of performing like the new models. They can provide so much more in the way of productivity, quality, and value that they appeal to the "gotta have it" emotion.

Today, the prospect should see you as a partner, not a hunter moving in for the kill. Believe it or not, potential customers expect to be closed—it is no mystery that a salesperson wants their business. It's simply a matter of methodology-establish trust and confidence before closing, as customers will stop you from closing if they are not sold yet.

Closing is commonly misunderstood as a tool used only for the end of a sale. In reality, only a fraction of your closing is done at the end. When phoning a prospect, closing is done to secure an appointment. During the appointment, closing is used to schedule a demonstration. Upon completion of the demonstration, you find yourself closing for the proposal, or the sale itself. It is important to realize that you need to determine the prospect's "hot button," or what the key is to closing each particular customer. Are they interested more in a good price, security, productivity, or in some other buying criteria?

Closing does not mean providing your customer with a magical "catch-all," line that when cleverly spoken will lead to the sale's finality. Closing is a process which requires skill and confidence. Some points to ponder when refining your closing skills:

1. Improve upon your product, computer, and industry knowledge

2. Listen empathetically

3. Constantly seek agreement

4. Seek commitment throughout

5. Stay positive and enthusiastic

6. Practice your closing statements—they work

Make certain that when closing you are direct and to the point. Don't make implications or sugar-coat what you want to accomplish. Speak clearly with a strong emphasis on the point you are trying to get across. A statement such as, "Are you ready to make a positive decision for your company with my state-of-the-art digital system?" is clear and precise.

Try at all costs to be sitting and not standing when you close because it is more comfortable for the prospect (and besides, it's easier to slide over the paperwork). The following lists of closes are effective for the digital revolution. Some have withstood the test of time while others are making their debut. While the name of the close is irrelevant, the execution is vital. Remember, though, the most important element of closing is that you have earned the right to do it.

3-step close: (closes don't have to be one witty line)
1. Can you see where this digital solution would save you money?

2. Are you interested in saving money?

3. Do you agree that now is the best time to start saving money?

FAB: Give a summary list of the features, advantages, and benefits that prove you have the better mousetrap. Finish off with a spreadsheet that accounts for the prospect's huge savings.

The Free Demonstration (Puppy Dog): Bring out a system so they "fall in love" with it, only this time let them know the value of the demonstration. Normally the delivery, set-up, and pick-up, along with free service and copies, can run up to hundreds, if not thousands, of dollars.

Testimonial (Reference letter or e-mail): Yesterday's reference letter may just be today's e-mail. Make sure you have a few on hand (laminated would help keep them from becoming tattered). References from those in the same industry as your prospect are especially helpful.

The Alternative Choice: This has been a very popular close for a long time—it gives the prospect a choice and when they choose one the deal is closed. "Do you want the digital system delivered at the end of this week, or the beginning of next week?" or "Would you like the saddle stitch finisher included or the standard one?" are two examples.

Yes: In phrasing your questions, pose them in such a manner that necessitates the prospect to answer "yes" to the majority (if not all) of them. Then relay the response. "It seems as though from all the "yeses" I'm receiving that this piece of equipment will fit beautifully into your company. Let's fill out the paperwork."

Internet: If your dealership, manufacturer, or even competitor offers product via the Internet, make sure you are familiar with the price, terms, and conditions. Get on the Internet or have this information printed out and show the prospect your value is better. You'll enjoy stating, "I thought the Internet was supposed to eliminate the salesperson and offer a better deal..."

Incentive: Provide the buyer with yet another reason to purchase your product. Time deadline incentives are effective, but only if the deadline is truly imposed. In addition, these must be put in writing (accessory inclusion, rebate, interest free, trade-in, or gift). These deadlines must be firm, because your credibility is ruined if you make contact after its expiration only to offer it once again.

Marriage Proposal: This is a heart-felt one with a smidgeon of nervousness, but is spoken from the heart: "Will you purchase this product from me?"

Ben Franklin: The pro and con list—it provides the customer with a list of advantages and disadvantages. Probably the oldest close used today.

Trial: Basically start with an "If I...then will you?" such as, "If I can show you this product and it meets all of your needs, will you fill out the paperwork?"

VP of Sales: Ask directly and firmly, "Are you ready to be closed?"

Contingent Order: "Let's fill out the paperwork and if the demonstration proves that this model will meet your needs completely we will just leave the unit" or "Let's fill out the paperwork and I'll take the offer back to management and fight for its approval."

Assumptive: Because you have satisfied every need and have sensed the customer's approval, you assume that the deal is complete. Try, "Let's look at a date for the installation." You may be surprised at how such a simple line can break the tension and seal the deal.

Often times, closing involves more than one person. If this is the case, it is most strategic to do it one at a time. After each contact has approved the purchase, use him or her as a reference with the next. When approval has been met with everyone involved, reassure each individual that their decision was a wise investment. If they wanted to hear a plain "thank you" they would have gone to the mall. A more powerful statement such as, "You made a great decision with your investment and I'll make sure that everything runs smoothly after the equipment is installed next week" is reassuring and welcome. Don't look at closing as the close of your relationship with the customer; treat it as a marriage.

Look at each close as a fresh new start in a relationship and work hard to maintain it.

Closing is an art that, when used properly, can be effective throughout all phases of the sales cycle. It is a great measuring stick when determining how the sale is progressing. Throughout each phase it provides an assessment of where the appointment is going—whether or not the customer is approving of the product you have to offer, and how it fits into their company's requirements. Once approval is gained, it provides a dialogue that facilitates the signing of the final paperwork. This paperwork signing leads to yet another valuable relationship that can provide you with additional opportunities (as well as references) in the future!

RUDY Says: Closing is done with confidence after you've "earned" the right. You accomplish this by meeting a customer's needs while gaining a commitment every time.

Chapter 13

Persistence

WHEN GROWING UP I WAS FORTUNATE THAT MY PARENTS instilled in my siblings and me many values, including that of persistence. We were taught to work hard and be persistent until we got what we wanted. My parents were persistent in their quest for a daughter, because you see...first there was Jeff, then Fred, then yours truly, followed by Kyle, Jaren, Jon, Derek, Matthew, and then *finally* Stephanie arrived! Now that's what I call persistence! My dad then had to depend upon his persistent nature to provide ten children (William Benjamin made his debut a number of years after Stephanie) with three square meals, along with seeing to all of his other financial responsibilities, not the least of which were college educations! It is this trait among many others that helped make my father one of the most successful salesmen in the history of the Prudential Insurance Company. Selling insurance for forty-five years requires a lot of persistence, which hasn't left him yet! He's still selling strong at the age of seventy and is listed as one of the country's top producers!

The biggest difference between people who succeed and those who don't is not usually talent (or lack thereof) but persistence. Many brilliant people give up. Who wants to run the risk of getting knocked down again and again? Abraham Lincoln, perhaps the most persistent person ever, stated, "I'm not concerned about how many times you have fallen, but how many times you get back up." Highly successful people don't quit. Often it's said that successful people are ordinary people who got up one more time than they fell down. Persistence is a trait that we're all born with; over the years it is sometimes lost as our confidence fades. We need to hold onto that trait that we displayed in the grocery store at the age of two as we kicked and screamed for the candy bar at the checkout. Hopefully we've tempered our kicking and screaming, but we still need that "Don't give up" attitude.

To rightfully be persistent you have to have motivation and confidence. Knowledge generates confidence, because you are fully aware of the benefits that your product can provide, and you are persistent because you are excited about how these applications will make your customers' operations run much more smoothly. Since office products have become digital, there is so much more to learn. Dedicate extra time to the learning of your products—this will give you a stronger belief in the solutions you are selling.

Persistence seems to come easier at those times following a successful sale. The confidence is flowing and you are feeling pumped up! It is at this time that you should proceed with calls and contact your toughest prospects, or make an additional fifteen calls to make up for a call volume shortage for the week. Being assertive is a fundamental sales trait, and as you gain confidence it becomes second nature. Yet it all starts with persistence.

Use the psychology factor. Tell yourself that everyone is a potential customer. This helps motivate you when making your daily calls. Everyone *is* a potential customer because the average office product system is replaced about every forty-eight months. You need to emotionally commit yourself each day to not give up, because staying power will give you paying power! Mentally predetermine activities that are important to perform during the day, from prospecting to closing.

Just as there is an emotional commitment, there is a scientific, analytical one to persistence. You need to be familiar with the degree of persistence required to result in the final outcome you are striving for. When prospecting, you should be able to schedule three to four appointments for every eighty telephone contacts and another six to eight for every eighty cold calls. With proper qualifying, the yield will be about three to four demonstrations, which will be one and a half sales in a week's time. If the numbers listed above seem unattainable, you're probably not pushing yourself throughout the entire day. Sometimes rejection and mistakes slow you down but remember, if you make a mistake, it's only a failure if you don't learn from it. You may find it necessary to set up a list of tasks with deadlines and a check-off sheet to ensure you obtain the calls necessary to succeed.

Your ability to be persistent cannot be dictated by an ominous mood or bad weather. Sometimes being "under the weather" can generate an unmotivated state of mind. Some days it seems as though more and more salespeople hit the pavement seeking that same piece of pie, and it's just too overwhelming; or after working diligently for eight hours only one person has agreed to an appointment. The reality is, it's a competitive world and like it or not, persistence has to overcome all of these obstacles. What's more, it has to happen every day, first thing in the morning, not just when you feel like it!

Being persistent is not to be confused with being "pushy." Pushy salespeople are rather bothersome, but persistent ones gain respect if they are relaying their ability to provide value to the prospect's business. For example, it's good to be persistent if you've discovered another value to relay to the customer. Just make certain this information is appealing and that you are able to generate further interest every time you call—this will practically guarantee that your calls will be taken. Once you call back "just checking in," you may have permanently worn out your welcome. It takes talent to know when *not* to call.

The degree of persistence you employ will vary with everyone. Yes, we all have to row with the oars we were given, but it's not the size of the oars that counts but how many times you paddle! Sylvester Stallone stated, "I am not the smartest or the most talented person in the world, but I succeeded because I keep going and going and going."

Or take one of history's smartest people, Aristotle, who said, "We are what we repeatedly do. Excellence then, is not an act, but a habit."

My father repeatedly stated, "The right habits will take you through the wrong times." Your ability to be persistent has to be consistent. It's difficult at times because we don't want to interrupt others during their busy day, but the show must go on. As your career grows, so will your knowledge, motivation, and confidence —all-important factors in the persistence arena. So...maybe you don't have ten children as your motivation for persistence, but you still need to exemplify this trait if you are to become a "successful seller."

RUDY Says: It's always too soon to quit. Do what you do not want to do and you will become what you want to be *if* you are consistently persistent. The race is not always won by the fastest runner but by those who just keep running.

Differentiate

This is where the stars are born. What will you do to differentiate yourself from the competitor to earn the sale? Everyone appreciates creativity, but that will take an investment of your time along with a strategy of when and how to implement it. The way you communicate to others may have to change as you get involved in major account deals. Finally, knowing how to manage your time and gain a reasonable profit is essential to make a high income while keeping your life on the sane side!

Chapter 14

Creativity

M<small>Y WIFE, KAREN, HAS THE GIFT FOR CREATIVITY, AND ONE</small> New Year's Eve she devised a plan for a most memorable evening for our two boys, Corbin and Brody. Included in the plan were accommodations that included a king-sized bed and private bath with a hot tub. The room included skylights, TV/VCR with unlimited movies, room service, and coupons for a manicure, pedicure, and backrubs. The best part was the room rate–free!

The boys celebrated the evening in our bedroom down the hall from theirs and it was the most fun they'd ever had. Creativity means simply thinking outside the normal lines. The expense is minimal to none and only requires that you be innovative in order to differentiate yourself from your competitor to win more deals.

Your creativity is what will set you apart from your competition. The buyers hear basically the same message from every salesperson they encounter: "We have the best product, our service response time averages four hours, and we have an aggressive price this month." If this sounds too familiar to you, then it's time to get creative!

When contemplating the purchase of a product, the buyer experiences two very different sentiments. The first is the facts, and just the facts. The other is emotions, or personal feelings. Throughout our careers we are trained on product and company knowledge but don't receive much training concerning how we can cater to the emotions of the buyer. Factual information can become so boring that it leads to the prospect's creation of spreadsheets on who has what specifications. When evaluations resort to this method, the product with the lowest price seems to win. Get away from this by injecting some creativity into each phase of the sales cycle, which will give your office products career some revitalization.

Even if you're inspired to be creative, it may be easier said than done. Creativity is definitely unique to each personality. What is suitable for you may not be so for the next salesperson. Only use a method if it is fitting and try to imagine yourself as the recipient of these ideas. How would you respond?

Prospecting

Get noticed by your prospect! What better way than to write a personal note on your business card (front or back) instead of just handing it over? Everyone likes the personal "handwritten touch," even in this day of sophisticated technology. Likewise for a mailing: Don't you open the handwritten letters before the pre-printed ones? Mail or pass out flyers that demand immediate attention, such as, "$50.00 reward for information leading to the sale of a digital imaging system." Don't be afraid to extend this offer to your customer base, or even your service department.

Another "attention getter": Send out a blank letter except for a P.S. (which everyone loves to read) at the bottom which states, "You are probably sick and tired of hearing every day how great everyone's product is. I saved you the time and went immediately into what is important...asking for an appointment with you to prove it!" Simply state that you will be calling soon to schedule a convenient time to meet. When you do call, the prospect will definitely remember your letter. If your call ends up in voice mails and is not returned, leave a message such as, "I'll sing my next message if I don't hear back from you!"

Investing a few dollars in "attention getters" when prospecting can pay off immensely. Take your business card and enlarge it various sizes up to 11 by 17 inches. During your cold call state, "I need your help. What size business card will it take to get an appointment to help your company out?" Making color copies of a flower and handing them out is another inexpensive way to gain attention and get results. If the account is worth a gamble send along a lottery ticket with a note, "Take a chance on me." Other examples of inexpensive items: Write on your business card, "You are worth a mint" and tape a small mint to the card (or flyer). Go down to your basement and recruit the toy soldiers and attach a note: "We will protect your office equipment..." or use a puzzle piece from an old puzzle you were about to throw away: "We're the missing piece." One of the very best attention getters I've seen (when all else had failed) was the handing out of a small colorful rock whose attached note said, "You think that this rock is hard, getting an appointment with you is even harder! I'll be calling you this week to see if we can "soften" your office equipment costs." Take advantage of any holiday to gain attention over the competition. If it's St. Patrick's Day, offer a promotion on a hundred dollar bill with a leprechaun's head instead of the president's. Valentine's Day is great for handing out real roses to key businesses. The list goes on and on for special occasion days.

If you sell in a large metropolitan area with spacious office buildings where there is a security staff, go attack them before they get you. Immediately ask to see the management firm of the building, and then ask them about renting a room for an open house. Next state that you need to invite (a polite way of soliciting) tenants in the building for the open house. The management firm may be willing to trade the rental fee for a small printer, copier, or fax. To ensure ample participation, have lunches catered in—put invitation flyers in all of the bathrooms advertising your "free lunch." There are many possibilities; use your imagination!

Appointment/Qualifying

Confirm appointments by fax, relaying a positive message such as, "I'm excited about our meeting today because I'll be bringing with me some ideas that will make your company more productive." Once the appointment is finished, give out a "certificate of appreciation" on the spot or e-mail/fax it to them when you return to the office. During an appointment use a sight seller and include the customer's company name and/or logo from the Internet. This demonstrates that you "walk the talk" on technology. Change the term "sales proposal" to "marketing program." Use the word "impression" instead of "copy," "output devices" instead of "copier," and "solution" instead of "sale." Using strategic words will differentiate you from the competitor and put the prospect at ease. Finally, when you quote the product you've recommended, also include the product one level higher. Everyone wants to compare and you never know when there is enough positive emotion to find additional dollars for the bigger sale.

Demonstrations

The demonstration process gives you the opportunity to let your creativity shine—it's your show! First, try using the word "free trial" before you set it up instead of "demonstration" because "free" is an emotional word that the public cannot get enough of. Let the prospect know this can be worth up to a one thousand-dollar value. When a new imaging system is delivered, installed, used for numerous images, serviced, picked up, returned, and depreciated, the costs can really add up.

Make the most out of the originals you choose by having them tell a story. When the images come out, point out some of the highlights that make you the best choice. It's also a great reminder to not forget anything. Use originals in your demonstrations that the prospect believes will be difficult to copy. Sometimes the worst originals are actually the best. Spill some coffee on an important document and then demonstrate how this tainted paper, once dried, will still feed and how your product will make the necessary adjustments automatically to produce a perfect copy. Create and store your own originals on the computer. That way you will always have a clean set to print out when necessary. By the way, if you print out something that is light, use it to show how your imaging system will fill it in with solid blacks. Print out the numbers one through twelve on separate pages to keep it simple with the customer when demonstrating duplexing and booklet making. Use the names of key personnel in your demonstration materials. Not only will this help enhance your memory of those attending your demonstration, but people enjoy seeing their names in print. Print out the prospect's "needs list," and use this as a checklist for the demonstration goals.

Another "attention getter" is to use paper that is torn and run it though the automatic document feeder, bypass, or cassette drawers to prove reliability. Finish the demonstration by stating, "I will copy the advantages of the competitors." Then proceed to copy this page of information the wrong way so a blank page prints out.

Another creative finish is to copy the lease and ask for the order (or if it is a digital copier have it already stored in memory and recall it).

Try to use color during the whole sales process. Color grabs and holds attention, improves understanding of material, emphasizes and helps locate information faster, makes comparisons easier, and adds professionalism. Utilizing newsletters that you have produced with various success stories and positive customer comments are also quite useful. Finally, make sure you laminate customer referrals on their letterhead (and keep them up to date).

You can see that creativity is limitless! Think outside the normal lines. You can do something as simple as asking your receptionist, "Which one of my customers is the most polite when they call in?" Give that person a telephone call, certificate of appreciation, or a small gift and make their day a great one! If you lose a deal, write a letter to the purchaser's boss praising how well the process was handled (even if it wasn't). Who knows, in thirty days another piece of equipment may be needed and you may get the call for your gratefulness. It is the creativity used in all phases of the sales cycle that will set you apart from everyone else. To know the facts is important, but it is how they are presented that will get the results we are all striving for!

One last way to be creative is to send an invoice to an individual you have just made a presentation to. The amount due may be zero, but you will surely get their attention. See the following page for an example.

RUDY Says: "Try it, you'll like it." Get in your "right" mind today and do something creative. It will increase your commissions while making your sales career more fun.

Bill To:

From:
Terrill Klett
6N830 Foxborough Road
St. Charles, IL 60175

Phone: 630-513-5306
Fax: 630-513-8802
tklett@aol.com

Invoice No.: 99065

Invoice Date: 03/08/02

Date of Service:
Drove to and from your business
| Time and mileage total | $65.00 |

| Appointment time 1/2 hour | |
| Includes Consultative Service | $45.00 |

| Total | **$110.00** |

Amount Due: $0.00

Thank you for the opportunity to
earn your business!
It was my pleasure, **please do not pay this**!

*Payment is not due unless you make a great decision
(which you are noted for) by investing in my product!*

Terrill Klett

Chapter 15

Communicating Effectively

PERHAPS MY PROUDEST MOMENT, OUTSIDE OF MY WEDDING day and the births of my two sons, was the day my wife granted me permission to purchase a riding lawnmower. My father had owned a nine horse-powered, err, boy-powered lawnmower and the size of our plush turf had been right at one acre. There was no gas, no oil...just the old fashioned blade powered by the sweat and strength of his nine sons. So, buying a mower with a seat and cup holder fulfilled my biggest wish in life.

After carefully shopping I arrived home excited one afternoon and proudly boasted that I had found my "dream machine." After my wife recovered from the dizzy spell that resulted when I divulged the price of my dream, she made me explain why it was worth a second mortgage. Because my mechanical ability is severely lacking, I could hardly repeat any of the words that described the features of my new friend-to-be. But I realized that the salesperson had communicated very effectively with verbal as well as non-verbal skills. From the facial expressions with a simple smile to the voice inflections that brewed confidence and enthusiasm, I had been taken (mowed) in.

In order to communicate effectively, you, too, have to know the various verbal and non-verbal skills to use. Research by Harvard and Stanford Universities has shown that eighty-five percent of our success is based on our ability to deal with people, and people are dealt with constantly on a verbal and non-verbal basis. Non-verbal communication strategies include facial expressions, eye contact, posture, gestures, dress, and overall appearance.

Verbally we communicate with our voices—our word choices, pitch, tone, and sound level. While we can definitely determine the words we will use, our pitch, tone, and sound level are not as easy to change. We are all born with a predetermined "sound" and there isn't a whole lot we can do to change this, but we can make an impact and add clarity to what we are saying by adjusting volume, pace, and inflection.

Why are verbal and nonverbal communication skills so important to our sales careers? Statistically, the average person remembers approximately fifteen percent of what they hear, twenty-five percent of what they see, fifty percent of what they see and hear, and seventy percent of what they say. The breakdown of personal expression goes something like this: Seven percent is through words, thirty-eight percent through the tone of your voice, and fifty-five percent through non-verbal skills (body language). Like it or not, deals are won and lost based on how you represent yourself, not necessarily on the product you are offering.

A strategic plan for implementing your verbal and non-verbal communication skills is fundamental in every phase of the sales cycle. While each phase requires all skills, as you progress through each phase you will need to be familiar with which ones are most appropriate at which time.

Appointments. During this stage, the nonverbal communication skill of professional appearance is paramount. Because you are meeting with the prospect for the first time, you are setting the stage for the future. Nancy Michaels, from Impressions Impact, wrote that we form up to eleven different opinions about a person within the first minute of meeting.

It is a fact—the more you are dressed up, the more you sell. Dress like a million bucks and others will think, "I need to hear what this person has to say." If you are just embarking upon your career in sales and haven't had the financial means to acquire such a wardrobe, consider purchasing a few moderately priced but professional pieces as an investment to be expanded upon later. Then top it off with a million-dollar smile, because studies show that people who smile are seen as more intelligent. In addition, smiling can detract somewhat from the focus on clothing. Smiling should be sincere and used as an accessory in your career, as well as in your daily life, and besides, it's free!

Eye contact is also vital and must be established immediately upon introduction. No one trusts the "shifty-eyed" salesperson so make sure you look directly into the eyes of your appointment for about three to four seconds. On the other hand, no one likes to be stared at, so look away often. Smiling should happen simultaneously with the eye contact and should continue if there are others to greet. This should all be done at arm's length.

Demonstrations. The non-verbal appointment skills are equally important here since you'll probably have first time acquaintances present. Your posture should be confident and professional—stand up straight with your shoulders back. Don't slouch or lean because this can exhibit laziness. When you discuss the paper drawers and finisher walk over or bend down to touch them. Don't point or use your foot to kick the bottom drawer.

Gestures are useful in your demonstrations to enhance the

showing of the product. The larger the group you are speaking to, the more you need to dramatize the movement of your hands and arms. Don't clasp your hands and avoid putting them in your pockets-this can easily advertise an attitude/look of nonchalance. Clear your pockets of keys, change, wallet—anything that may be distracting to those watching the demonstration. Don't overdo it on the jewelry, either, as this could detract from the product you are trying to show.

Closing. When you are asking to close the deal, it is your professional, non-verbal appearance that is critical. Your authority, as well as your knowledge and integrity, are all working together at this point. The facial expressions you portray should reinforce what you are saying. Depending on the prospect, you may have to put on a concerned, serious, smiley, or poker face. Eye contact should be direct and sustained until your point is established. You need to set the tone when it comes to a closing statement because your livelihood is based on bringing back orders to the office.

Prospecting. Articulation and professional appearance are the two most important items of concern. Good articulation means you speak clearly and coherently. By your pronunciation of sounds, syllables, and words, you are establishing a reputation of knowledge and intelligence in regard to your product and how you are perceiving the needs of the prospect. If you are not perceived as being articulate by the prospect, you may be perceived as unprepared and uncertain about what you are selling. Speak slowly to avoid slurring words.

Dressing professionally when cold calling will also add to your credibility. While the rules on what is considered appropriate business attire have relaxed somewhat, a jacket and knee-length skirt for women and a two-piece suit for men still can't be topped. Dark colors, such as black, brown, navy, or charcoal gray, are the best bets for men and women. If you plan a day in the office to make telephone calls, dress is not as critical but don't get too casual because you may end up feeling too casual on your calls.

In all aspects of your selling career, *act confident even if you are not.* The nervous "butterflies" in the stomach are all right; just make sure you have them flying in the same formation once the adrenaline takes over.

It's no secret that the world we live in is filled with those who are judgmental, critical, and short on time. You need to take advantage of every minute you have by using effective verbal and non-verbal skills. Spend some time practicing using your voice, face, and body language. You need to establish an advantage over the competitor in the buyer's eye. Confucius stated, "I hear and I think. I see and I remember. I do and I know." Your customers make thoughtful decisions on what they hear and see you do. By communicating effectively, you can sway those decisions to favor you and what you are selling.

RUDY Says: Act confident, even if you are not. The first impression may be from the outside but the lasting impression will be of your heart.

Chapter 16

Major Account Selling

LANDING "THE BIG ONE" IS DEFINITELY CAUSE FOR CELEBRA-
tion, and no doubt is one of the most exhilarating events in your
office products selling career. It's a personal assurance that
you've arrived, that the countless hours spent training, prospecting, and preparing have paid off. You've laid the groundwork and
established a relationship that can cultivate the best references in
town, if you play your cards right.

National accounts are normally headquartered in your territory
with locations throughout the country or a particular region. Major
accounts reside basically within your serviceable area. In addition
to national accounts, the other large opportunities that exist are in
government purchases and bids. These can be frustrating,
because often times it seems as though the bid winner was the
salesperson who made a math error.

Major account selling can pay off substantially, but these opportunities don't arise every day. It is your ability to balance these large
potential opportunities with those of a smaller, steadier pace that is

vital to maintaining your desired income. The smaller thirty to ninety-day cycle business needs to be intact as you spend time penetrating the longer-term six to twelve-month accounts. If the short-term selling has not been successful, you may find yourself pressuring the large accounts, which will be obvious to them. Because establishing a healthy rapport from the beginning is imperative, being overzealous at the improper point could ruin your chance of establishing the long-term relationship and financial payoff. Patience is a virtue especially here, because these accounts are a great potential source of ongoing business and revenue.

Dealing with a more sophisticated customer necessitates a more sophisticated sales consultant. To determine if you are wired to be successful in the major account environment, honestly ask yourself the following:

1. Are you able to manage delayed sales gratification?

2. Do you have "executive" presence and intuitiveness? Some customers may want a chameleon-like personality to mirror them, while others may not want as close of a relationship.

3. Are you strong in the organizational skills department? Can you be efficient while not being redundant? Create the tools upfront such as the presentation, proposals, and letters. Once created you can use their basic format over and over, tailoring them only slightly to fit each account.

4. Product and program knowledge should be second to none.

5. Do you have what it takes to persevere?

Intuitiveness is critical if you are to succeed in selling to the major accounts. It's a mind game that can pay off if played correctly. You must be able to identify through the eyes of the major account what qualities they are looking for in a vendor and sales person. Most often the account is looking for a reliable partner, not an office products company. When they are experiencing difficulties in their facility two thousand miles away, they want a solution and quickly. They need a salesperson who will come through for them and not pass the buck, one who will display the empowerment necessary to make the decisions and arrangements that will expediently resolve the issue at hand. Major accounts need a sales rep to follow procedure, give straight answers (no beating around the bush), and to understand their business, all the while showing some flexibility in their daily dealings. Passing the buck and attempting to oversell are two traits that won't be tolerated with "Mr. Big."

From the beginning, you must initialize a thoughtful game plan—one that can see you through from start to finish. First, a database of potential accounts must be established. Resources are numerous. Try internal accounts, Dun & Bradstreet (D&B), city and state directories, referrals, public information sources, social networks, and the Internet. With this list, important data fields can be identified and used in your contact manager software package. Proceed with a phone call to each account requesting an annual report. This report is vital not only for the contact information, but also as a source to determine the direction the company is heading, such as possible expansion plans or even changes in technology.

Your next call should involve a little probing into exact contact personnel including titles/positions. Scanning, color products, digital copying, printing and faxing can involve various avenues into the account. You should become familiar with everyone involved, even the assistant's assistant! After you've established in your mind the "who's who" of the account, you need to begin the activity of perseverance:

✓ Identify and complete all "bidders" list or proper paperwork as required.

✓ Send out introduction letters utilizing their terminology of important aspects of their applications based on their annual report. Some of this may be posted on their web site.

✓ Place follow-up telephone calls to set up appointments.

✓ Send a thank-you letter, even if you did not get the appointment.

✓ If the prospect is ready to meet with you, begin choosing your selling team.

✓ Your introductory presentation should contain lots of technology without too strong of an emphasis on product. "Light" selling is the norm.

✓ Ask them to evaluate the product, even if they are not in the market at this time.

✓ Present a professionally bound, outlined marketing plan (proposal).

✓ Your corporate presentation should include solutions to more productivity and cost savings.

✓ Close and Implement.

Each account will vary depending on their policies and procedures. Some may require site surveys, Request For Bid (RFB), or a negotiating session. Know the politics of their decision-making process. Don't be surprised if the contact you've been pursuing abruptly leaves the position, only to be replaced by another who is uninterested in the progress you've made with their predecessor in an effort to show you who's the new boss. In this situation, it is the contacts you've successfully established on your way up that will recommend you as a key player to this new individual.

National accounts will consider many vendors and after intense evaluations will narrow their choices to two or four. In all likelihood, by this time you will be familiar with exactly which ones are in the running. The competition will no doubt be stiff because you may be up against a selling team that includes ranks from the president to an experienced network consultant. Make sure you take measures to differentiate yourself: Prepare on-going newsletters, host an open-house in which food is served, or entertain with a golf outing, ball game, or theater show. When meeting face to face, be sure to include lots of technology talk and present them with a total "marketing program" designed specifically to their needs. Your standard sales proposal won't suffice. This creative plan will include references on the local and national levels and should be printed on company letterhead (and even laminated). Creative thinking will give you the competitive edge against the competition.

Landing a major or national account is a lot of work and takes plenty of time. By progressing systematically and thoroughly you are bound to win them over. Keep a keen eye on the details. If you find a certain niche application, run with it. Many accounts are won because of the discovery of one feature. The strategies to succeed necessitate a level of professionalism not usually required in standard accounts, but can bring you to a new level in your career, because the sales can keep going and going and going...

RUDY Says: Take off your short-term hat and put on your long-term one by selling the program and not the price. "R & R" is the key—*Relationships* make it pleasurable for the account and *Reliability* of the equipment makes them happy!

Chapter 17

Gaining Additional Gross Profit

THE ENGLISH LANGUAGE SEEMS TO BE NONSENSICAL AT times because there are words that, though spelled identically, have entirely different and unrelated meanings. When examining the much sought after gross profit, immediately my mind associates the word "gross" with something disgusting or crude. Of course, profits are anything but gross in this context, but what is gross are the low margins that are taken today by a desperate sales person. Gaining additional profit can be a mutually beneficial situation for you and your customers, as each deal must be profitable for you to continue in your sales career. What's more, the fact that you are gaining additional gross profit means that customers gain an experienced representative who will be able to provide them with the various solutions they will require in the future.

The key component in obtaining those larger profit margins is product knowledge. You can't sell a connected segment four system without knowing about networks. You can't sell a facsimile with Internet capability without knowing about e-mail. Finally, you can't beat out the competition if you aren't capable of fully educating the prospect of their weaknesses. People buy knowledge because it exudes confidence in their choice to buy from you, as well as weakens their desire to dwell solely on price. Profit is a direct result of the extra time invested in increasing your knowledge of the industry.

Gross profit is not a one-shot deal; it encompasses planting seeds throughout the entire meeting with your prospect. It is critical to establish the groundwork the first time you meet. Statements such as, "We represent (manufacturer's name), which is a high technology manufacturer with outstanding features and quality that normally isn't the lowest price" or "Would you like to know why it's better to invest a few more dollars a month than you may had planed to make sure you get exactly what you need?" Everyone wants a good deal but, more importantly, they want the right solution.

Your product's value and how the buyer perceives it are paramount. Let's suppose that you and your competitor have a segment four digital imaging system with the exact same list price of $26,995. Without even demonstrating the system, your competition quotes a discounted price of $19,995 and your quote remains at the list of $26,995. Because the system hasn't been demonstrated, as of yet, price isn't the final issue. Initially, in the buyer's mind, the more expensive system must be of a higher quality and more capable of meeting their needs. As the sales cycle progresses, you may end up quoting the lower cost, but the tone of a more quality product has already been set, and the buyer is pleased because they've purchased the "better" product at the same price. Don't discount prematurely and definitely not too generously, because often times it's not even requested. The focus from the start has to be on providing the right solution for the customer, not over concern about your competition and their price.

The "top-down" selling technique should be used when appropriate, normally during an appointment or demonstration. This entails using or quoting as many accessories as possible. Initially, a quote should include the best finisher, extra paper cassettes, memory–items that would provide top-notch productivity resulting in the greater cost. The philosophy behind "starting big" is that your result will either be that of agreement or a decision to eliminate those features that are not essential for the application. Psychologically, since the price is being decreased, there will be a lesser push toward the buyer seeking additional discounts. The cost reduction by elimination of features is also much more tolerable than starting at a minimum and building from there. If the system price is determined initially, be sure that the profit margin on the added accessories is higher. Once the decision is made upon the product, adding accessories lowers the customer's negotiating power. If software is added, there generally should be no discounting.

Hints for gaining additional gross profit:

✓ Know the difference between price and cost. Explain to the prospect that while the price of the equipment may be higher, the overall cost will be lower because the product is more reliable with less downtime. Factored into cost includes future trade-in value, training availability, supply costs, and service response times.

✓ Just say "No." Buyers have become more educated and are trained to "beat you up" for price. Often times this behavior demonstrates that there is definitely interest and the deal is in the works. When a prospect wants to negotiate further, act shocked and let them know that you've already been through the ringer with them and that enough is enough!

✓ Use the word "promote" rather than discount.

✓ Use the word "invest" instead of "cost."

✓ When you finally quote prices, don't use numbers that end in "99" or "95," because they can trigger the buyer to assume that there is "fluff" in your quote.

✓ If you leave the prospect believing that you can discount even more, they will go for it.

✓ With in-house demonstrations, the margin is usually higher because the buyer won't feel as powerful or aggressive. To promote a favorable mood, make sure you provide a gift for coming or have food catered in.

Adding dollar values to the features of your products may also generate more profit, especially if the competing product is without them. When you first educate yourself on a product, you learn the feature, advantage, and then benefit (FAB). Add to this the fourth letter, an "S" for "savings." Let the prospect know the dollars they can save with each key feature. For example, the cover sheet feature on a facsimile is not generally requested by a prospect, but can definitely be used to create interest. A business that faxes one hundred times per day could electronically send a cover sheet, therefore eliminating 100,000 sheets of paper over four years. If each cover sheet is now produced from a copier or printer at an average of 2.4 cents, the savings ("S") is approximately $2,400–all from just one feature! Pick four or five features on your next training session and work out the dollar savings, and don't be shocked when you see these savings amount to the tens of thousands of dollars over the lifetime of the equipment you are quoting!

When submitting a proposal, always include a section that includes the "upgraded" model. It's natural for curiosity to be aroused as to the next level higher and the cost involved. Be sure to include a statement that you are informing the prospect of this upgrade for "comparison purposes only." Most customers appreciate having this information handy when making their decision, and many times the customer will choose to purchase the upgraded model, especially if you can explain the extra productivity benefits as well as their return on investment (dollar savings per month).

Not long ago, when the sales rep was moving a "box," it was much easier for a buyer to insist on the lowest price possible. Today, office product sales involve providing a solution accompanied by a support team. If you've impacted your customer correctly, they may just be a little fearful of *not* selecting the service and or product you're offering. Buyers don't want to jeopardize crashing their network system or slowing down their paper flow because the decision was made to purchase the cheapest offering. As a sales rep, once you've arrived at being an "expert," you can be bolder in keeping a better margin. Everyone wins that way, and you'll be the one invited back with the next technology change!

RU**D**Y **Says:** Look at profit as a two-way street. The more your customer profits from your effort and knowledge, the more you profit in commissions. Show a lot of enthusiasm and believe your product and service is worth the price you charge.

Chapter 18

Defeating Time

THERE WAS ONCE A TOUCHING ADVERTISEMENT IN THE reward section of a newspaper that said, "Lost yesterday, somewhere between sunrise and sunset, two golden hours, each set with sixty diamond minutes. No reward offered, for they are gone forever."

The time thieves are robbing us every day, and it's time to fight back! Most statistics say we waste two to three hours a day, which equals about nineteen weeks, per year! Wow! Imagine what you could do with nineteen extra paychecks every year! This alone is incentive to better budget your time.

In the office products industry, it is the timesaving features that you are trying to sell to prospective customers. Given this, why is it that we have such difficulty in managing our own time in our workday? With an analysis of your day and some practical planning, you'll be well on your way to finding and budgeting your time to be most successful and productive.

First, evaluate your schedule to find "unproductive" and

"wasted" time. Unproductive time is spent driving, filing—any of those tasks that can be important but should be saved until the appropriate time. Prime sales call hours should be spent pursuing prospects and attending sales calls. Wasted time is just that...wasted! For example: You arrive at the office at 8:12 a.m. and grab a coffee all the while chatting with a co-worker for just a few minutes before getting started for the day. In its totality you have already wasted about thirty minutes! Don't accept those unnecessary personal phone calls, and politely dismiss the co-worker who loves to "drop by" for a few minutes each day to chitchat. To track your time and the amount that is wasted, record the actual time you start and finish your workday. Create a sheet entitled "Interruptions for the day" and record each minute spent on personal telephone calls and "drop-ins." At the week's end total those minutes and identify the main culprit. You may find some much needed changes to be made in this area.

Next, make a list of the activities that make you the most money. These activities are, for the most part, time spent in front of the customer in appointments and demonstrations. Take the wasted time that you have already identified and use it in an activity that will get you in front of a prospect.

The old school of thought, the one that supposes success can only be accomplished with long and hard work, is not necessarily so today. It's what you do with those hours-managing your time, prioritizing, and working hard—that formulates success. Stephen R. Covey identified this in his book, *The Seven Habits of Highly Effective People*. He places time into two categories: Effective time and efficient time. While efficient means doing things correctly, effective is where you want to be. Effective is spending your time in the areas that will generate the best results—the high payoff activities. Dale Carnegie and Zig Ziglar have also stressed the importance of these two words.

Effective vs. Efficient: On Friday afternoon you can be efficiently making telephone calls for four hours until 5:00 p.m., but it's not very effective due to the fact that most decision-makers aren't available at this time. It would be most effective to make the calls in the morning. Not only would the likelihood of reaching the decision-makers be greater, but they would also be in a better mood knowing that the workweek was drawing to a close. The call is also more non-threatening when you ask, "Would the beginning or end of the week be better for you?" (when phoning on a Friday), as this seems like your appointment is a longer way off than it really is.

Determine what your schedule will be for each day and actually write down what you would like to accomplish in the order of importance. See the "Weekly Planner" and "Weekly Goals" on pages 110 and 111 for an example of how you might do this. This planning will only take you about ten minutes, but can save you hours. Block off time to make phone calls, planning, training, or whatever, but always stay focused. This may mean declining phone calls for a certain period of time. The idea here is to make sure you concentrate on the task at hand. Becoming involved in too many tasks at one time makes you distracted and much less productive, which means less concentration and more time spent trying to get back "into the groove."

In this list of accomplishments for the day you should always include appointment confirmations. Arriving at an appointment only to find it postponed or cancelled is a huge time thief. Confirm appointments by fax or call and ask for voice mail. I have found that communicating by fax is an ideal method because it makes it more difficult for the customer to have a change of mind. Write a very positive note on your fax such as "I'm excited about meeting with you today! I'll be bringing with me some ideas that will make your company more productive." You can include in the message that you'll be out all day, but if a reschedule is needed to contact your voice mail. When confirming by telephone you may consider asking for their voice mail to eliminate the live call and possible cancellation of the appointment.

But in spite of your best efforts, all of us are going to experience some unproductive time because it is unavoidable. It's everywhere! Utilize this time wisely. It can be turned into educational time. Sixty million baby boomers commute to work averaging forty-four minutes of travel (183 hours per year) at least five days a week. There is a plethora of cassette tapes available that we could all benefit from listening to during this time. Stock up on these sales as well as motivational tapes, which can be obtained for no charge from your public library. When waiting for appointments, you can be reading similar materials or returning phone calls if appropriate.

The computer has also become a deceptive thief of our time. Delete the games that come preloaded. Control the use of the Internet by avoiding "surfing" away from your schedule for the day. Return personal e-mails during the evening hours.

But also make time for some fun. Set a deadline and, if accomplished, reward yourself. Rewards can be as simple as a coffee break or a walk outside to freshen up. Taking a well-deserved break in front of your boss is enjoyable when you both know the effectiveness of your workday. To make deadlines you may have to learn how to say no. You can't be all things to all people all of the time. Deciding what not to do is just as important as deciding what to do. Eighty percent of the results you achieve are from twenty percent of the work you do.

Don't let the time thieves rob you anymore of the precious "diamond" minutes and "golden" hours—fight back! Start today with one change and watch the gold in your commissions grow. Henry Doherty, a great Industrialist, said, "I can hire men to do everything

but two things: Think and do things in the order of their importance." Let's show the Industrialist era that with the "digital" era,
you can do both!

RUDY **Says:** You can never get back time so make
the most of each "diamond" minute and
"golden" hour. Cherish them like they are the last ones
you'll ever see.

Weekly Planner

Week of _____   Name _____

Item	Monday	Tuesday	Wednes.	Thursday	Friday	Total Points
Telemarketing Goal 16 per day 80 per week 1 point each	☐☐☐☐ ☐☐☐☐ ☐☐☐☐ ☐☐☐☐ Goal 16 pts Actual ____	☐☐☐☐ ☐☐☐☐ ☐☐☐☐ ☐☐☐☐ Goal 16 pts Actual ____	☐☐☐☐ ☐☐☐☐ ☐☐☐☐ ☐☐☐☐ Goal 16 pts Actual ____	☐☐☐☐ ☐☐☐☐ ☐☐☐☐ ☐☐☐☐ Goal 16 pts Actual ____	☐☐☐☐ ☐☐☐☐ ☐☐☐☐ ☐☐☐☐ Goal 16 pts Actual ____	Weekly goal 80 points Actual ____
Cold Calls Goal 16 per day 80 per week 2 points each	☐☐☐☐ ☐☐☐☐ ☐☐☐☐ ☐☐☐☐ Goal 32 pts Actual ____	☐☐☐☐ ☐☐☐☐ ☐☐☐☐ ☐☐☐☐ Goal 32 pts Actual ____	☐☐☐☐ ☐☐☐☐ ☐☐☐☐ ☐☐☐☐ Goal 32 pts Actual ____	☐☐☐☐ ☐☐☐☐ ☐☐☐☐ ☐☐☐☐ Goal 32 pts Actual ____	☐☐☐☐ ☐☐☐☐ ☐☐☐☐ ☐☐☐☐ Goal 32 pts Actual ____	Weekly goal 160 points Actual ____

Add .5 bonus points for each cold call in which you get more information than just the name of the decision maker

Item	Monday	Tuesday	Wednes.	Thursday	Friday	Total Points
Appointments Goal 2 per day 10 per week 10 points each	Company _____ _____ Goal 20 pts Actual ____	Company _____ _____ Goal 20 pts Actual ____	Company _____ _____ Goal 20 pts Actual ____	Company _____ _____ Goal 20 pts Actual ____	Company _____ _____ Goal 20 pts Actual ____	Weekly goal 100 points Actual ____
Demonstrations Goal 3 per week 25 points each	Company _____ _____ Goal 25 pts Actual ____	Company _____ _____ Goal 25 pts Actual ____	Company _____ _____ Goal 25 pts Actual ____	Company _____ _____ Goal 25 pts Actual ____	Company _____ _____ Goal 25 pts Actual ____	Weekly goal 75 points Actual ____

Add 10 bonus points if this is an in-house demonstration (closing ratio goes way up in-house)

Add 40 points for each order _____   **Weekly goal: 415**
60 points if it is connected _____   **My Total _____**

Weekly Goals

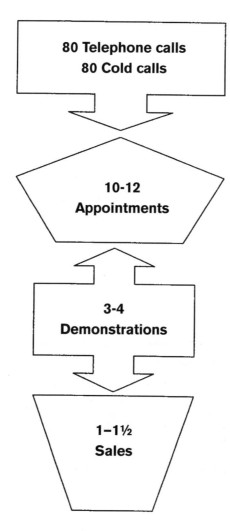

Activity	Points	Gives Approximately
Telephone Calls	80	3-4 Appointments
Cold Calls	160	6-8 Appointments
Appointments	100	3 Demonstrations
Demonstrations	75	1-1½ Sales
Totals	415	

(If you get busy delivering, installing, and training because you reach the 1–1½ machines per week, the points should still come out to about 415 because you receive anywhere from 40 – 60 points for each order.)

Chapter 19

The Price War

"**I**T'S NO GOOD, IT'S NO GOOD" EXCLAIMS THE BUYER, THEN off he goes all the while boasting about his purchase. The buyer downgrades the quality of goods being offered until the sale is final, and then claims to have gotten the best of the deal.

Does this sound familiar? The above quote and description were taken from Proverbs 20:14, in the New International Version of the Bible. If it is any consolation to you, salespersons have been getting beaten up over price for thousands of years. The price war will continue for thousands more, so be prepared to handle it.

Price is second only to oxygen in terms of importance during the sales cycle. If you do not know how to handle it precisely, you will be gasping for air. Today, price is an even more critical issue because of the lack of trust in our society. We are constantly being informed of rip-offs, scams, and switches—just tune into your local news. Buyers have a fear of paying too much just as you do when shopping for a major purchase. When price is mentioned, a veteran buyer has the attitude of, "Sure, now what is the *real* price?"

The buyer today is educated not only in how to get the best price but in the technology changes that are rapidly taking place. In many instances, they know more about the networking and digital environment than the salesperson, which means they can take control of the appointment from you.

Get ready...you need to be prepared to enter this battle. The first key is to build trust with your prospect. The third and fourth letter of trust spells out "us." If the prospect feels you are in it exclusively for the sake of a commission, no trust will be built. If you portray yourself as a caring consultant with genuine interest in helping their business, trust will automatically be built. I love the saying, "People don't care how much you know until they know how much you care." Rob Troxel, a veteran of twenty-five years in sales training, states in each of his basic courses, "The key is to build value in you and the product or service because in the absence of value, price is the only thing!"

If you are not allowed to build trust or value, guess what—no deal or no profit. Many times with office products, someone wants a price without even meeting with you. I have even seen occasions where the prospect (if you could call them that) said to fax or e-mail the price to them and not to call! It is amazing... and even more amazing is the salesperson who does it! No trust building opportunity here!

The strategies for handling price are numerous and you need to have confidence in your ability to portray to the prospect that you and your product deserve a fair price. The market area you work in also dictates how you would go about handling price. Don Amsden, owner of Lafayette Copier in Lafayette, Indiana, states, "In our market you do not play games with price. You go in with your best price right away because if you come back later with a lower price, the buyer will throw you out."

Major markets seem to be more flexible with the "pricing game," so you need to develop strategies to handle it professionally. One strategy is to attack price *before* it is brought up. Do this by stating, "Normally my product is an investment of a few hundred dollars more, and our sales with this model have never been better... Would you like to know why?"

Another, more direct, method is to give the price right away to see if you are in the ballpark before everyone's time is wasted. This is especially helpful when someone is looking at a low-end piece of office equipment.

Price really is unimportant when you are asked prematurely. When this is the case, you can say positively, "I do not know! I do not know until I find out exactly what your applications are. Then I need to determine the type of accessories needed to optimize your productivity." Another reply would be to give a range such as, "Our products range in price from $1,000 to $50,000 depending on your needs. Is that the range you are in?" Finally, a response is, "I am glad you are concerned about price. Even if my product were free today it probably would not do you any good if it does not meet your company's needs. Please allow me to review exactly what you are doing so that I may put a plan in place to give you the *exact* price you are looking for." Remember to respond enthusiastically and get right back to your presentation without delay.

Fun answers are effective, but you must possess the type of personality that can pull them off. When the "What is the price?" is asked too early, you can reply, "Way too much at this point...because you have not yet seen any value to my product."

Related to this is, "The price is too high" from the customer, to which you agree, "Yes! It is way too high right now. As soon as I can show you the benefits of my product you will see that it is not too high."

Other fun replies have been around a long time, such as,

"Good things are not cheap and cheap thing are not good" or "Pay now or pay later."

Another strategy is feeling out your prospect during the first qualifying appointment. Ask the question, "Is the product (or service) you offer the lowest priced in your industry?" Normally, you will get the answer that it is not with an explanation of why. Take this answer and bank it and if the price issue comes out later, explain why you are not the lowest using the reasons the prospect said (if they are applicable).

What if the prospect demands the best price right away? There are two ways to handle this. First, the wrong one, is to give it to them. Second, the correct way, is to give it to them (you did read that correctly). The real issue should not be the final price right now so give them your "first" best price. You may end up going to a second or even third "best price."

What do you do when it looks hopeless because the purchaser says price is the *only* thing that is important and you are too high? Desperately, but with confidence again, challenge them and pull out an order form and say, "Great, let's write up the order for one dollar less than the best price you have now" (as long as you are comparing apples to apples). Proceed to pull out an order form and state, "After you sign this I will submit it for approval." Guess what? You will find out that the problem was not one hundred percent price, which is good, because you probably could not have closed the deal anyway. You did accomplish, though, victory over the price objection and will possibly now be able to uncover the real objection.

Most of your prospects will appreciate your presentation and the value of your product, and even though you have established a trust with them, they will still "beat you up" on the price issue. That is good—you are in the game! Remember that the buyer is paid by his company to make the best decision at the best price and is trained to motivate you to sharpen your pencil. Don't be afraid to say your pencil sharpener is broken and re-state your value!

RUDY Says: Price is determined from the performance of you and your product. Always be ready for the price issue to arise at any point of the sales cycle.

Yourself

Plain and simple, you have to succeed for yourself because no can do it for you. All the reading of books (even this one), listening to tapes, and practice at the office won't do you a lot of good until you perform "live" out in the street. Some days will be very painful and others will offer jubilation. You'll be pushed and pulled in many different directions from your customers as well as your managers. As your success builds, there will be danger in you becoming complacent and taking shortcuts. Motivating yourself consistently is a difficult task but is necessary in order to sustain a successful sales career. The future technologies will definitely change, but will you?

Chapter 20

The Painful Journey...Success

Growing up surrounded by eight brothers created a natural environment consisting of many physical confrontations! Minor brawls meant merely a few pushes, but when my parents were not in the near vicinity these fights could escalate and consume many hours, resulting in a disheveled house. Enter my father, upon completion of a grueling day of sales. He had no patience to endure the endless interviews required to identify the original perpetrator. Instead, any involvement whatsoever earned a direct ticket to his bedroom where he would inflict upon each participant a spanking. His words were plain and few. Spoken without emotion, he would matter of factly ask, "Who would like to go first?" Believe it or not, each of us wanted to be first, because we wanted our punishment and pain to quickly be over with.

As we matured (physically), my dad resorted to another form of punishment, the mental one. He would lecture us about our character and poor judgement—this was much more painful than those earlier physical punishments. Now, as we gather as a family for

119

various reasons, we reminisce and even laugh about the physical pain and mental anguish suffered, but we all agree that we learned our lesson and in the end, it was worth it!

Like growing up, to become successful in your sales career you must endure many painful experiences along the way. Most assuredly, the rewards will come but not until these "lessons" have been learned, and most the hard way. The earlier in your career you realize and address this, the quicker you'll find yourself residing in a thriving career. Get it over with—face the harder challenges early on to shape your succes—because the longer you wait the more painful it can become. What characterizes "pain" in the office products environment? A number of factors contribute. No recognition, criticism, anticipation of those larger commission checks, having to rise early, traffic, time away from family, the loss of a big deal, and even changes in technology. In addition to these, you can always rely on the two daily and prominent pains: Failure and rejection.

No one fails on purpose; it just comes with the territory. More importantly, if you aren't failing, sometimes you're not exerting enough effort. IBM, one of the largest technology companies in the world, was founded by Thomas Watson who said, "The way to succeed is to double your failure rate." Every failure means you are closer to a success. Thomas Edison was asked why he persisted after he had conducted and failed on more than five thousand experiments. His reply was, "Young man, you don't understand how the world works. I have not failed at all. I have successfully identified five thousand ways that will not work. That just puts me five thousand ways closer to the way that will."

It's perfectly acceptable to make mistakes on the telephone, have a bad appointment, and to lose a deal as long as you continue to give one hundred percent. If you lose a deal, ask the person why or what you could do differently next time to earn their business.

Rejection is unavoidable but the manner in which you react to it will be your barometer for success. After hustling in your territory all day only to be bombarded with rejection makes it difficult to arrive back at the office with a positive demeanor and engage yourself in your last ten telephone calls before calling it a day. However, using Edison's theory, every rejection you experienced during the day brings you closer to a "yes." Always go for it because failure is a direct result of giving up and no longer trying. Never turn back—no matter how difficult the task at hand. If Columbus had turned back no one would have blamed him, but of course no one would have remembered him either. Will your name be referred to and remembered at your company one day?

Success is such a broad term, and there are varying degrees that characterize it. When have you achieved success? With the constant exposure to the worldly view of success, we are told, "When I have this...then I'll be happy." It's this, that, or the next thing. In sales we tend to use the dollar as the measuring stick of success, which is a problem in itself. There is nothing worse than "fooling" yourself into thinking your bigger wallet makes you a better person.

When my two boys were younger I took them sixty miles north-west of Chicago to Donelly's Wild West Town, which was a town set up as it would have been in the 1800s. One of the activities in town was panning for gold. Never mind that the gold being sought after was fool's gold, because at their age anything gold and shiny was good. I noticed that as the contents of the bags increased, so did their excitement and happiness. They actually began comparing the contents of their bags with those around them because everyone was going for that large bag of gold. When I reminded them at the end of the day that their "gold" was worthless, their sense of satisfaction disappeared.

Be careful not to let your sense of satisfaction reside in the tangible moneybag, as this can lead to the dreaded SADF disease—Short Arms/Deep Pockets. Ironically, we go through a life that can include, at times, painful strides for more money, which can end up being the biggest pain of all if it leads to negative character changes. First set your sights on your health, safety, and good relationships, because your financial success can be temporary and it is your significance that matters in the end. Periodically, take the time to ask yourself, "When was the last time I contributed something to someone else unconditionally?" This is not to say that financial success and your efforts to attain it are unimportant, but it is the manner in which you achieve those goals and your attitude toward those that you meet along the way that count. The measurement for significance comes in the end, when you have reached the finish line standing in the company of many others and are not alone. Such a feat can only be accomplished by becoming less interested in yourself and becoming a little more interested in those around you.

Pain, failure, and rejection are all necessary evils that you will encounter throughout your journey to success. Expect these obstacles and don't let them weigh you down. This industry is introducing fancy products and new technologies daily, but don't count on these to make you successful. It will take a large dose of hard work, the type that typified the industrial era, to reach your goals. Finally, when you do "make it," don't get too wrapped up in yourself because doing so can make a pretty small package.

RUDY Says: There is truth to that all-familiar aphorism, "No pain, no gain." The good news with pain on the job is that it becomes more manageable the second time around. Get it over with and start out the day believing and tomorrow you'll start achieving.

Chapter 21

Got a "Match"—
Sales Management

BUILDING A COMPETENT, SUCCESSFUL SALES TEAM IS EVERY sales manager's goal. The responsibility of achieving this status for your team rests solely upon the sales manager's shoulders and nobody else's. A team of this status does not develop overnight—it takes time to establish all of the key elements that would produce the all-star sales force.

Managing people today is much more difficult than it was fifteen years ago. Today much more is demanded of your time by the sales staff. You need to be much more flexible and adaptable to the personalities of those on your team. Each person is motivated differently, and to become successful at your job you need to be able to pinpoint each individual's motivation and go with it. It used to be that your focus was adjusting to the environment of the customer, but now you must even become chameleon-like in your own office. You have to consider the members of your team as individuals, and adjust to their own individual needs and motivations.

In interviewing new salespeople, try to get to know them as well as their expectations for the position. If you ask a salesperson what they want out of their job, the number one response is "good income." Because of this desire for financial success, the initial plan is to present an outline that details goals, and a strategy that facilitates the salesperson's attainment of this "good income" goal. Sometimes a new salesperson has visions of an income that are unrealistic and, if so, this must be pointed out right away. This unrealistic expectation could result in income expectations that are too high or not quite high enough. A strategy must be determined to cover either.

The response, "Plenty of opportunity for challenges" runs a close second. This business is very challenging today as it is, but some reps want to excel in the "recognition arena" and will take on other responsibilities to earn it. Perhaps they can provide computer training or research the competition through the Internet. A "challenge list" is always a great motivator. However, at the same time, this desire needs to be monitored in such a manner that prime sales time is not being spent here.

The third factor on the "want list" is job security. Even though there is a lot of shifting of the worker today, human nature has built in us a security desire. Other items that sales managers must be aware of today are recognition, training, genuine concern of management for its people, promotional opportunities, pleasant working conditions, and autonomy.

Once a sales rep is on board, a mutual respect must be established. The sales manager can earn respect by knowing all of the traits of a successful salesperson and then teaching those traits. This is more difficult today because there is much more to teach, which means more time training and coaching and less time selling. Today a sales manager can't know it all like many (including my former "street" manager Jim Van De Veire)used to. Since time is limited, make sure that you lead by example. Remember the old adage, "The mouth can lie but the body can't"? If you require the sales team to begin each day promptly at 8:00 a.m., then you start at 7:45.

During the initial ninety days of employment, responsibility lies solely on the manager of the new salesperson. Make sure the new sales reps are familiar with the schedule of daily activities and expectations. They should know that a lot of prospecting and training will be taking place, in turn leading to the rewards (commissions) from months four through twelve and beyond. Bringing new people aboard is an expensive undertaking. The investment can run anywhere from $2,000 to $20,000 with a single new salesperson. Therefore, this is a critical period and must be meticulously handled to result in a good return.

Sales meetings offer opportunities for your leadership abilities to shine through. You are on center stage and have the attention of all your staff—be creative. One or two meetings per week are sufficient and should be scheduled at about the same time each week. Monday mornings and Wednesday late afternoons seem to be popular choices. Consistency is important, because having to reschedule appointments by sales staff could create resentment, but most assuredly will be inconvenient.

The meetings should last about forty-five minutes to two hours, depending on content, and should start promptly. Don't wait for late arrivals because this will waste time for the remainder of your team. Make sure the sales team knows ahead of time what you are covering so they can arrive prepared or bring in additional information.

It used to be that management's job was to challenge the employee-to keep them on their toes. Today it is the employees who are presenting management with challenges of their own, most often very selfish ones. How about the attitude of, "What can my company do for *me*? What do *I* get? I have the education or talent and am owed big bucks."

Me, me, me! It used to be that sick and personal days were rarely taken. Now it is second nature to take advantage of them all and, as a manager, you need to adjust to this new generation of workers. Once a salesperson's track record is proven, this conceited attitude is almost tolerable, as long as they keep producing.

In the final analysis, sales managers no longer live to "light the match" under sales reps and throw them out the door. Today that "match" can be considered the ability to identify each team member with the eighty-twenty rule. Management and employees should be able to agree on about eighty percent of the job. The remaining twenty percent is where managers can work to match up better with their sales reps, and they shouldn't expect this twenty percent to be handed over to them. What is important to sales managers may not be what's important to their reps.

The ability to "match up" can be obtained with mastering some basic human skills. When criticism is in order, it is important that the message relayed is that the performance is being criticized, not the performer. Lost sales are lost sales but are also a learning experience for the rep. A great scholar once said, "The two greatest fears of all people are the fear of receiving criticism and fear of receiving advice." Remember to take a daily "PIT" stop with your team: Praise, Information, and Training. These are always welcome so be sure to give them a daily dose. Recognize their strengths in a group session, rather than just individually. Recognition is easy to give out and doesn't cost a thing.

If you could identify in one phrase the primary responsibility of sales management, it would be "Improvement of sales staff's productivity." Leadership, motivation, and knowledge are all excellent qualities, but if productivity is lacking, changes will have to be made. Hopefully, if all has gone well, you may reach the paradox stage of "hanging on by letting go." You can hang on to your best salespersons by giving them more freedom. Trusting your subordinates is a flattering form of motivation. This not only builds you a stronger, more confident, sales team, it frees you up to accomplish bigger tasks.

Sales reps need to use their managers for brainstorming periodically. Managers aren't employed to sit at a desk until an appointment or problem arises. Take time to set up a weekly salesperson-sales manager appointment to ensure everyone is on the same page. Ideally, the success of the relationship would have the salesperson working their hardest when their sales manager is not around.

Managing a sales staff takes major effort and creativity. From the ability to adapt to your employees' personalities to presenting them with ongoing challenges, it is the driving force behind a successful staff. Though exhausting at times, it is always rewarding. There is nothing more enjoyable than reviewing the members of your team and then looking at the high volume of sales you have all attained together. Being a part of a successful team such as this makes life exciting, and the next obstacle around the corner worth the challenge!

RUDY Says: Good management is what happens when you're not around. The best managers manage the least. Make an effort to be flexible with the last twenty percent of your expectations.

Let's Get Rid of Management

People don't want to be managed. They want to be led. Whoever heard of a world manager? World leader, yes.

Educational leader.
Political leader.
Religious leader.
Scout leader.
Community leader.
Labor leader.
Business leader.

They lead. They don't manage. The carrot always wins over the stick. Ask your horse. You can *lead* your horse to water, but you can't *manage* him to drink. If you want to manage somebody, manage yourself. Do that well and you'll be ready to stop managing. And start leading.

AUTHOR UNKNOWN

Chapter 22

Gaining Customer Loyalty

IN *HOW I RAISED MYSELF FROM FAILURE TO SUCCESS* (1949), Frank Bettger relayed his discovery of the secret to success with potential customers: "Finding out what people want, and helping them get it." More than fifty years later, the story line hasn't changed, only the names and places.

With all of the current advances in technology, it can be much more complicated to find the appropriate office product solution, which in turn makes it more difficult to maintain a customer base that is loyal. Today it is too easy to shop around and change products or the companies who supply them. The customer can obtain any product specifications over the Internet and there are numerous publications that rate and compare products. There's hardly a customer left who isn't afraid to comparison shop by contacting a competing dealer or manufacturer. However, strategies exist that can minimize most of the "betrayal" and can help you retain the accounts you've worked so hard to establish.

First, we need to understand where the loyalty has gone and

why it has diminished. The answer lies within two factors: Technology changes and customer fears. When technology changes, customers are up for grabs because it's difficult to determine who has the advantage. If you propose a connected $20,000 digital imaging system to a current customer, common sense would dictate some research and shopping around. The mindset has been that technology is changing daily, so the newest information out there must be studied first. (The good news here is that opportunities for new sales reps in our industry have never been better—all customers are fare game! Major accounts that had established themselves with their suppliers used to stay put, but are now much more open to alternatives.)

Because the buyer's options are wide open, the factor of fear sets in: The fear of making the wrong decision. Today that fear is magnified because we are dealing with the network, and if a problem erupts, the entire company can become aware of it. When repair service used to be required on the analog copier, it was for the most part expected and was not a reflection upon the purchaser. The thoughts racing through the buyer's mind today are, "How do I know this is the best product for our network? Will it cause my network to slow down, and what kind of support will I get with the network?" You may have had excellent service in the past when the copier broke down, but the customer is now wondering if you can equal the support when the network experiences a difficulty. Those worry-free days of just re-ordering a replacement analog copier are long gone.

How do you meet the challenges of creating a "safe" decision in your relationship with a customer? The most vital requirements in establishing such a relationship are time, talent, and knowledge. Not only do customers need to know that you are completely informed about your products and how they work in their environment, you have to be able to usher in the right people to provide solutions. Just as important is your follow-through and dedication to honoring a commitment that you've made. We all get busy and it's easy to delay a task that won't result in a commission check, but don't hope that the customer forgets about a task you promised—just do it!

Jim Cook, perhaps one of the most successful office products salesmen in Chicago over the last twenty years, affirms that consistency plays a key role in gaining customer loyalty. "I always return calls quickly, no matter if it concerns a complaint or interest in purchasing a new product." Cook adds, "I call to be proactive and don't wait for the complaint." Every salesperson's goal should be to establish such a relationship with the customer that if a mistake is made, they are confidant that you'll be there to remedy it. With larger accounts, just expect the problems to be more numerous. This is fine because these problems are actually opportunities to demonstrate your skills and follow-through. Remember, if you take care of your customers, they will take care of you.

Never assume anything with a customer and do be proactive with your relationship. Don't be afraid to give your good customers a short five to six question survey on dealings with you and your company. Ask the tough questions, such as, "Was the office equipment we installed three months ago less, equal to, or more than what you expected?" "Have I returned your calls promptly and answered your questions completely and accurately?" "Is there anything we can change within our company guidelines to service you more efficiently?"

Questions of this type will not only minimize the chances of losing future business, but also impress upon the customer that you really do care. It takes months to find a customer but seconds to lose one, so know what your customer expects ahead of time.

Bill Gates in his book *Business at the Speed of Light* states,

"Your most unhappy customers are your greatest source of learning." Don't be afraid to contact the customer base that has been lost in the last few years or those who are on the edge to determine what the problems were. Statistics show that if you promptly resolve a complaint, the majority of customers will do business with you again, whereas an attitude of indifference gets you nowhere and in fact is the number one reason today that customer's find alternative suppliers.

New customers are the best source of new business. Why? They are excited to have a new office product and want to tell others. Make sure you contact them right after the install and inquire as to whether they know any others looking for a similar product, or if you could use them as a reference. Take it a step further by offering to draft the letter yourself and have them print it on their own letterhead. This makes it effortless for the customer and can result in many gains for you.

Customers want to be taken care of, and would like to show loyalty because it is very time consuming to shop around. Loyalty is more convenient for them, and they want to like and trust that you will be open, honest, and vulnerable. Each customer is unique in its loyalty of buying, and your job is to figure out what this is. Are they buying the need for security, admiration, power, recent technology, or name brand? Once you uncover their "hot button," your success will be determined by your versatility of adapting to their style and need.

To establish and maintain a customer base that is loyal to you is not easy. Like any relationship it requires time and effort, but customers respect a knowledgeable salesperson and one who is consistent. By being attentive to your customers' needs and leaving the impression that you genuinely care about how they are being taken care of, you are relaying to them that you value them as customers. Establishing their loyalty is sure to follow.

"It takes twenty years to build a reputation and five minutes to ruin it."

WARREN BUFFET

"We can do no great things, only small things with great love. Give until it hurts."

MOTHER TERESA

RUDY **Says:** The difference between a problem and an opportunity is often nothing more than a point of view. With your customers don't *act* sincere, *be* sincere. Anyone can sell a product, but few can genuinely give their hearts.

Chapter 23

Danger!–Complacency

_____

DURING MY LAST VISIT TO THE ZOO, I COULDN'T HELP BUT think that these animals really have it made when considering their counterparts living in the wild. Take the lion for example–it appears that he really is the king. Every day healthy, balanced meals are served to him, personal trainers are at his beck and call, and medical professionals are available to him, with all expenses covered.

For the remainder of the lion species not fortunate enough to have such posh accommodations, life truly is a jungle. They must fight for their very survival every day. They are in competition with each other in a territory for status, recognition, and nourishment.

It would be easy to assume that the zoo lion has it made, but this is not necessarily so. Because of the zoo lion's manmade habitat, he is not challenged–complacency characterizes his mood and therefore he becomes physically and mentally weak, which will eventually result in the loss of his keen inherent senses. The lion residing in the jungle is working his territory every day, which sharpens those senses he was born with, making him stronger and more capable.

Our choice to reside in the office products "jungle" is actually one that is making us stronger, sharpening our knowledge and skills to survive in this environment. Because of intense competition and rapidly changing technology, we are constantly forcing ourselves to learn more and strategize differently to win the sale. The jungle is good for us, because if we're not constantly challenged we become like the zoo lion—complacent and eventually weak in our abilities and desire to succeed.

Complacency is the satisfaction with yourself and your accomplishments. It can sometimes be associated with conceit. Arrogance sets in, especially if your budget or quota is attained in excess monthly. This is dangerous because you start believing that as long as you attain your quota, anything is okay. Next, you become comfortable with your current situation resulting in some laziness and soon the desire to excel diminishes. These problems are all familiar to me, as I too once traveled this path. The following memo, written by my Regional Sales Manager at the time, Fred Eddy, and dated November 30, 1992, helped lead me to the evil path of complacency:

> "Please join me in congratulating Mr. Terrill Klett for his fine efforts during the fax sales contest held during the first half of this fiscal year. Terrill's strong efforts and persistence have once again paid dividends. Terrill is our winner and has earned a free vacation to Japan. It should be noted that Terrill seems to win almost all the contests. Maybe we can all learn something from his accomplishments. As Terrill has, let's all continue to strive to become more professional and of greater value to our customers. Through that type of commitment we will all gain greater worth and begin to challenge all comers for the "top prize." Once again, congratulations to Terrill on a great job."

I was at the top of my selling game but my adventure on the path to complacency was beginning. I started thinking like the zoo lion in that I should be catered to more often. Everything seemed perfect until a year later when I was summoned into the personnel department to account for my unacceptable behavior. I was initially in shock because my territory still resided in excess of 100 percent. Some of the skills outlined earlier in the book, teamwork, listening, and attitude had been slowly fading away without much of a notice to me. The lack of my desire to change was very obvious to others and my company had made the tough but correct decision to address it.

In spite of myself, I had become dangerously comfortable. I should have listened to an ex-army veteran who once told me that the first page of the U.S. army survival manual stated, "Comfort will kill you." Even Will Rogers had the answer when he said, "Even if you're on the right track, you'll get run over if you sit there long enough." It took a hundred-ton train to run me over before I realized I had fallen into the lion's trap. When you become complacent, you become replaceable.

We all need to evaluate our complacency status from time to time. Are you thinking that "Things around the office aren't what they used to be" or do you have an attitude of "Nobody is going to tell me what to do"? When training is scheduled, do you find that you are "too busy" and have you lost the desire to put extra time in because "It's not worth the effort now"? Is bringing in new business a waste of time because it will only backfire on you and result in a quota increase next quarter? Have you begun setting your first appointments for the day around 10:00 a.m. rather than 8:00 a.m. because it makes for an easier day? Do you feel that you have little or no competition with your product or marketplace?

If you have responded favorably to any of these traits, the complacency bug has bitten you. You can run, but you cannot hide from the truth, so you need to bite off a little humility, make the admission, and then put forth the effort to combat it! You can start today by spending more non-selling time educating yourself with computers, networking, additional sales skills, and digital technology. Change the manner in which you work your territory; schedule an early or late appointment.

There are remedies for complacency. A Fortune 500 survey of executives stated that flexibility (being able to change) was one of the top four character traits that were pertinent when hiring new employees. This is encouraging, as are the other remedies for a complacent attitude:

✓ Remember how you got to the top. When you started out you believed, and when you *believe* you can *achieve*.

✓ Work according to the direction of your employer and/or customer–it doesn't matter what worked in the past. Today's guidelines will change again and again so acclimate to changeability.

✓ Keep prospecting; cold calls will keep you mean and lean.

✓ Volunteer all the time. Be the first to raise your hand when someone has to research a subject, give a presentation, or demonstrate a product.

✓ Ask someone in the office that you respect to keep you accountable and give you feedback on how you are progressing.

✓ Look at the last six months and compare the new business brought in to the account base. Shoot for a fifty/fifty split.

There is no doubt that complacency is dangerous. At the same time it can be a powerful career builder. You may believe that the fifteen years you have experienced in your sales career is substantial, but it could be that you've actually repeated one year fifteen times.

There is an old sports quote that states, "There is room at the top, but not enough to sit down." If you are at the top now don't become complacent and sit down, because you'll become comfortable and have difficulty getting back up. Selling office products is not what it used to be, so make the necessary changes to "beat your best." It's a jungle out there in the office products sales arena; truly, it's survival of the fittest.

Change is upon us—
it is inevitable.
It is disturbing when done to us,
exhilarating when done to us.
It arouses anxiety when we don't
know how it will affect us,
brings opportunity when we plan
and get ready for it!

AUTHOR UNKNOWN

RU**D**Y **Says:** As long as you are green you are growing; as soon as you are ripe you start to rot. Don't let complacency rot your office products sales career. It makes "cents" to change!

138

Chapter 24

Are You "RUDY" for the Future?

"THERE IS NO NEED FOR ANY INDIVIDUAL TO HAVE A COM-puter in the home." Such an outlandish statement but, nevertheless, it was a declaration made in 1977 by Ken Olsen, President of Digital Equipment Corporation. Most assuredly he felt very strongly about this at the time, but how times have changed! Some days I wish Olsen had been correct. I see my boys spending a considerable amount of time on the computer, downloading information (games mostly!) and printing them from the Internet with fifty percent fill on each page. Whatever happened to the good old whiffel ball and bat?

On the other hand, no doubt the younger generation will be a considerable asset to the salespeople of the office products world. Demands of speedy and elaborate printing consisting of multitudes of colors, coupled with the nonchalance of leasing payments lasting forty-eight months and the desire to have the latest and greatest, are most assuredly in our favor. The only uncertainty is the means in which these demands will be met. Gaining popularity today in garnering leads is the Internet. Demonstrating, qualifying, prospecting, and even buying are but a few mouse clicks away. Hopefully this will only be a supplement to the business brought in first hand from the old fashioned sales field. But the new generation of decision makers is maturing in an e-commerce world and utilizes the tool of the Internet to shop, compare, and purchase.

How far we've come! Printing as we know it today began in Europe about five hundred years ago. Prior to this, everything was copied by hand or printed from wood blocks carved manually. Then, in Germany in about 1440, Johanne Gutenberg and his associates invented the printing press, resulting in the rapid spread of the ability to read and write. It wasn't until 1938 that Chester F. Carlson, an American physicist, invented electrostatic copying. Working for the Haloid Company (which in 1961 became the Xerox Corporation), Carlson developed a dry process called xerography. This process was finally "perfected" with the birth of the plain paper copy machine in 1959.

Every year the office products industry becomes stronger and more interesting. Jeff Smith, Director of Consumer Services for Buyers Laboratory Inc., stated that the copier/document-imaging industry results in a twenty-eight-billion-dollar business in North America alone. The industry consists of eleven different copier manufacturers as well as nine more vendors who manufacture printers only. There are between eight and nine million installed copiers in the United States, which bear an expected life span of five to seven years. About 1.2 million new copiers (digital imaging systems) are sold each year. Interestingly, Smith also added that most of the 500,000 used machines that turn over annually are shipped to Latin and South America.

Due to the ever changing, increasingly complex digital technology and computer, we actually know less and less about more and more. Even if the typical workday of eight hours were to increase to twenty-four, this still would not allow enough time to keep up with all of the e-mail, voice-mail messages, and technology changes for the day. Like the farming days of the past, take one day off and you can experience a major setback, perhaps as long as a week! Is digital the future of office products or just a small blip in the technology metamorphosis?

Earlier predictions, especially in the late 1970s and early '80s, had the computer age heralded as the "paperless office." "Office automation" was the buzzword and environmentalists were cele-brating at the thought of the trees that would be saved. However, with the availability of electronic documents, more and more paper is being consumed today. Lou Slawetsky, president and founder of Industry Analysts, Inc., credits the "touchy-feely" along with the lack of confidence in the electronic solution as the justification for the mass paper consumption. "It's ironic that every technology we introduced to eliminate paper usage generates the need for even more. We're using fifteen percent more paper per year, which means we double usage every six to seven years." Slawetsky summed it all up when he said, "There will be a paperless office the day there is a paperless bathroom!"

Even the definitions of words in our language are not what they used to be! To my poor farming great-grandparents in Wisconsin, "log-on" meant something that was placed in the hearth to fuel the fire. To my grandparents, "modem" was something that you did in the hay field the week before. To my parents, "laptop" was reserved for a special time with the lucky kid of the night, a chance either to sit on Mom's lap to read a favorite book or in Dad's case to play "horsy," all the while holding on tight so as to not get bucked off. God only knows how our everyday words will evolve once my kids are grown and have families of their own.

Change is happening! Making discoveries on your own is

always more exciting than what someone else discovers for you. *Selling Office Products Successfully* will only initiate your race of discoveries. Chapter One introduced the concept of making a "choice" to change and succeed. If you weren't convinced then, I hope RUDY and the rest of the book have motivated you to be a part of the greatest industry in the world!

RU**D**Y **Says:** Times really are changing. Instead of me ending with "Good luck and have a nice day," I must sign off with "Please visit my web site at www.sellingofficepro.com."

"I learn more from originals left on the copy machine than I do from the employee newsletter...Isn't this a great industry!"

TERRILL KLETT, 2001

Ready – Understand – Differentiate – Yourself